▲ ▲ ▲

Helping
Teens
Stop
Violence

This manual is dedicated to Erica Sherover-Marcuse and Harrison Simms, educators whose teaching, vision, and example as allies of young people inspired this book page by page, sometimes word by word. In loving memory of you, Ricky and Harrison.

HELPING TEENS STOP VIOLENCE

▲ ▲ ▲

A Practical Guide for Educators, Counselors, and Parents

by

Allan Creighton
Director, Teen Program
Battered Women's Alternatives

with Paul Kivel
Co-Founder, Oakland Men's Project

with contributions from
Harrison Simms
Carrie McCluer

Hunter
House

Selections of this curriculum may be reprinted with permission
from Battered Women's Alternatives
"Talking About Sexism and Sexist Violence: Working Assumptions" page 23 adapted from
Erica Sherover-Marcuse, "Towards a Perspective on Unlearning Racism"
"Thoughts on Class" page 50 adapted from *Men's Work: How to Stop the Violence that Tears
Our Lives Apart* © 1992 by Paul Kivel, Hazelden/Ballantine

Library of Congress Cataloging-in-Publication Data
Creighton, Allan.
Helping teens stop violence : a practical guide for educators, counselors, and parents /
Allan Creighton, with Paul Kivel : with contributions from Harrison Simms, Carrie McCluer.
—2nd ed.
p. cm.
Rev. ed. of: Teens need teens. Concord, CA : Battered Women's Alternatives; Oakland, CA :
Oakland Men's Project. 1990
ISBN 0-89793-116-5 (pbk.) : $11.95. — ISBN 0-89793-115-7 (spiral bound) : $14.95
1. Social work with teenagers—United States. 2. Teenagers—United States—Abuse
of—Prevention. I. Kivel, Paul. II. Creighton, Allan. Teens need teens. III. Title.
HV1431.C74   1992
362.7'68'0835—dc20   92-23349

Cover design by Kristin Prentice, Sphinx Graphics
Book design by Qalagraphia
Project Editor: Lisa E. Lee
Editor: Jackie Melvin
Production Manager: Paul J. Frindt
Publisher: Kiran S. Rana
Set in Palatino and Helvetica by 847 Communications, Alameda, CA
Printed by Griffin Printing, Sacramento, CA

Manufactured in the United States of America

9 8 7 6 5 4 3 2   First edition

ACKNOWLEDGMENTS

This material was produced through years of education and counseling for adolescent youth provided by Battered Women's Alternatives (BWA) and the Oakland Men's Project (OMP).

Battered Women's Alternatives is the authority on domestic and dating violence in Contra Costa County, California, operating since 1977 to provide counseling, shelter, legal support, living skills training, and job placement for battered women and their children. The BWA Men's Program is the largest program for batterers in the United States. The Teen Program provides comprehensive education and support services for youth dealing with abuse. They may be reached at:

BWA, P.O. Box 6406, Concord, CA 94524
Tel. (510)676-2845

The Oakland Men's Project is a multiracial community-based violence prevention program, operating since 1979, dedicated to eliminating male violence and promoting cross-gender and cross-racial alliance. Through education with youth and adults and community organizing, OMP reaches high school and junior high adolescents, parents, social service professionals, and religious, civic, governmental and correctional organizations throughout the state of California and across the country. They may be reached at:

OMP, 440 Grand Avenue, Suite 320, Oakland, CA 94610
Tel. (510)835-2433

Special thanks for thinking and direction to Toni Taylor, Kristy Brodeur, Katie Krichbaum, Jenny Mish, Tracy Cuneo, Isoke Femi, Hugh Vasquez, Beth Kivel, Rebecca Isaacs, and Steven Wisbaum.

Funding for the original version of this book was provided by the Office of Criminal Justice Planning, the State of California, and the San Francisco Foundation.

LIST OF CONTENTS

Introduction ix
A Note to Parents xi

Section 1. Preparing to Work with Teens 1
  I Remember When I Was a Teenager
  Adult-Teen Questions for Facilitators
  Working With Teens
  Adults as Allies of Teens
  The Basic Agreements

Section 2. Liberation Theory and Practice 12
  It's About Power
  Power Shuffle
  Power Chart
  The Cycle of Violence
  Nonpower Visualization Part 1
  Nonpower Visualization Part 2
  Talking About Sexism and Sexist Violence:
     Working Assumptions
  Men Stand-Up
  Women Stand-Up
  Racism
  People of Color Stand-Up
  Whites Stand-Up
  Out Proud: Unlearning Heterosexism
  Coming Out Roleplay
  Closeness Dyad
  Thoughts on Class
  Adultism
  Adultism Visualization
  Teens Stand-Up

Section 3. Being in the Classroom 62
  Teaching as an Activity
  Goals and Process for Workshops
  Myths and Facts: One Method That Doesn't Work

Section 4. High School Program on Family and
            Dating Violence 81
      Before the Class
      High School Program Outlines
      Two-Day High School Presentation Script
      Father-Son Roleplay
      Act-Like-A-Man Box
      Party Roleplay
      Writing About a Personal Experience of Violence
      Act-Like-A-Lady Flower
      After School Roleplay

Section 5. Workshops 98
      Teen Oppression and Unlearning Adultism
      Unlearning Sexism
      Unlearning Racism

Section 6. Teen Support Groups 104
      What Is a Teen Support Group?
      Some Thoughts About I-Statements
      Support Group Agreements
      The Support Group Leader Alliance
      What Does a Support Group Leader Do?
      Group Safety
      Setting Up the Support Group
      Support Group Agenda Ideas
      Protocol for Reporting Child Abuse

Appendix 136
      Writing About a Personal Experience of Violence
      Group Sign-Up Form
      Group Invitation Form
      Parental Consent Form
      Support Group Agenda Form
      Using the Teen Information Form
      Teen Information Form
      Teen Program Pretest
      Student Survey (Anonymous)
      Teen Program Posttest
      Teen Program Posttest on Family/Teen Violence and
          Program Evaluation
      Participant Evaluation
      Follow-Up Teacher Evaluation

LIST OF EXERCISES, ROLEPLAYS, AND AGREEMENTS

I Remember When I Was a Teenager 2
Adult-Teen Questions for Facilitators 3
Teens Need Adults to 8
The Basic Agreements 9
Power Shuffle 14
Power Chart 16
Nonpower Visualization Part 1 21
Nonpower Visualization Part 2 22
Men Stand-Up 26
Women Stand-Up 27
People of Color Stand-Up 34
Whites Stand-Up 37
Coming Out Roleplay 48
Closeness Dyad 49
Adultism Visualization 56
Teens Stand-Up 57
How Adults Can Stop Adultism 59
Goals and Process for Workshops 72
Father-Son Roleplay 86
Act-Like-A-Man Box 87
Party Roleplay 88
Writing About a Personal Experience of Violence 90
One Thing 91
Act-Like-A-Lady Flower 91
After School Roleplay 94
Support Group Agreements 112

INTRODUCTION

This is a guide for adults who work with and care about young people. The material is primarily designed for educators and counselors; the message is important for parents and families as well. It represents the Battered Women's Alternatives (BWA) Teen Program's years of contact with adolescents in high schools, residential centers, correctional institutions, and churches, and those among our own volunteers.

We wrote this book to support the liberation of young people from violence. We believe that individual acts of violence are actually expressions of much broader patterns of social violence, and that social violence is an expression of long-standing power imbalances between "have" and "have not" groups in our society. What we see from day to day are the high percentage of individuals involved; what we rarely hear about are the broader imbalances that motivate the violence. To prevent violence, even to intervene in it effectively, we must ultimately turn our attention to rectifying the imbalances themselves.

This book is organized in five sections. You can go directly to Section 4, our hands-on curriculum for teaching young people. Or, beginning at the beginning, you can look at general issues for adults to consider in work with youth (Section 1); basic theory about age, gender, and race-related power imbalances which cause violence (Section 2); techniques for liberatory teaching (Section 3); the curriculum itself (Section 4); suggestions for training other adults in workshops on these issues (Section 5); and finally, beyond the classroom and workshop, strategies and techniques for setting up and conducting long-term support for young people dealing with abuse (Section 6). In every section we include exercises and roleplays for work with youth across lines of age, gender, and race. We suggest you try them out yourself and use them to train volunteers in these areas prior to classroom, workshop, and group work.

At the heart of the book is our own workhorse, the two-day, fifty-minute class curriculum on family and relationship violence prevention. The roleplays, exercises, and guided discussions in the book reflect years of experiments, consultations, trial and error, accidental and expected mistakes, as well as planned and lucky successes. Above all, they reflect the spirit of young people and adults who are learning to talk together in order to face, resist, and stop the violence.

This book also includes alternate versions of this basic curriculum which allow you to adapt it to different time constraints and, in particular, to offer a 3-day workshop incorporating the BWA video on dating violence, *My Girl* (ordering information is at the back of this book). All of the curricula are designed to be presented by adult and youth volunteers with a modicum of training. This is a "how-to" manual for getting into the classroom and *beginning* the discussion; we believe strongly in the ability of youth and adults to keep the discussion going.

Finally, the book gathers reporting policies, tests, written exercises, permission slips, and classroom tips we have developed as we have built our program.

We invite you, as you use this book, to keep in touch with us. The BWA Teen Program and the Oakland Men's Project (OMP) are available for consultation, problem-solving, and strategizing about what works and what doesn't. It is only in our interchange that we will begin to end the violence that brought us here.

THE FOUNDATIONS OF OUR WORK

The four components of all our work with young people, adults, and each other, whether in classes, workshops, support groups, or meetings, are:

Safety

Healing

Liberation

Justice

Working for justice is part of our liberation process. Freeing ourselves from oppressive violence is clearly liberation. Healing from past hurts and our culture's conditioning process is essential for liberation. And in all of our work, establishing safety with each other is the prerequisite for both healing and liberation.

A NOTE TO PARENTS

It is not easy being a parent, even in the best of times and circumstances. Today, in the face of massive cutbacks in jobs, benefits, education, childcare, and other family support, it is more difficult. It is harder yet for those of us who are single parents, stepparents, lesbian or gay parents, or who live in interfaith or multiracial families. Emotional support for parents, high-quality and low-cost childcare, and financial support for families are as nonexistent as ever. On top of all this is the reality of family and community violence that we must prepare our children to face.

How do we support young people who want to make choices and resolve conflicts using alternatives to violence? How do we give them the information they need, the benefits of our experience, and access to resources, without either overprotecting them or controlling them?

This book can help by showing where to start. It identifies the violence that young people face in their daily lives. The best way to address these issues is through the experiences you have in common with your children. Neighborhood and family events and relationships, the news, movies, and music—each of these provides countless opportunities to listen and talk about violence. Current family dynamics and past experiences with abuse, sibling relationships, falling in love, money, childraising practices, cultural background, jobs—these are also topics which raise issues of violence with young people.

Our focus in this manual is on how we as adults can be more powerful allies for young people. The goals are listed on pages 59–61, "How Adults Can Stop Adultism." Start by reading through these goals. Make a commitment to being a strong ally for young people, and think about what this will require realistically.

Beyond this commitment, we need to identify what we as adults still carry with us from our *own* experiences of adolescence so that these do not get in the way of our being in healthy relationships with young people today. You can use the exercises on pages 2 and 3 —"I Remember When I Was a Teenager" and "Adult-Teen Questions for Facilitators"—to begin. Next we suggest you continue reading through the articles in Sections 1 and 2. If you have a partner, or friends who are parents of adolescents, you might want to talk with them about the material in these articles. Supporting young people means supporting ourselves and each other as well.

After reading the articles look through Section 6 on support groups, particularly page 114, "What Does a Support Group Leader Do?" The ideas on "I-Statements" earlier in the section are useful for families as well. You might then want to look through the Support Group Agenda Ideas on pages 121–129 for ways to talk with young people about difficult subjects.

Section 3 on education can be useful in understanding what young people face in most school settings. Section 4 is a school-based curriculum to use in the classroom. Reading through it will help you learn how violence is learned and passed on. Section 5 adds more focused workshops you can also use. You may want to help organize a local group to do these presentations with young people, or you could help set up support groups such as those described in Section 6.

Young people are often eager to talk, if they are respected, listened to, and not threatened. However, if there is a history of emotional, sexual, or physical abuse in your family, then this must be addressed and healed first. If there is a history of silence, denial of problems, or avoidance of difficult issues, it will take time for young people to believe that you honestly want to change those patterns. Trust builds slowly. After all, there are few, if any, places where young people can feel safe from adult power. Be patient and honest. Don't promise more than you can provide.

Despite our best efforts, some young people will take risks, including life-threatening ones. We can help them see the choices they have. Beyond that, sometimes the only thing we can do is to let them know that we will be there when they need help or want to talk with us.

Be creative. There are probably other young people besides your own children whom you influence. They all could use you to support their safety, healing, and liberation. This book will enhance your efforts to do so.

Section 1

Preparing to Work with Teens

Unity Photo: Alan Kondo ©1992

This section addresses important questions for adults who work with young people: what was life like for me as a young person, and how is my experience likely to affect my exchanges with young people now? We begin with two questionnaires, "I Remember When I Was a Teenager" and "Adult-Teen Questions for Facilitators." Work through these exercises before you read the article "Working With Teens" and the tips for adults who want to be allies of teens. The section ends with the basic agreements we make with both young people and adults at the beginning of all our work.

▲ I REMEMBER WHEN I WAS A TEENAGER

Please briefly answer the following questions:

1. My favorite kind of music was _____

   My favorite radio stations were _____

   My favorite D.J. was _____

2. The clothes I wore the most were _____

3. My best friend was _____

4. The biggest crush I had was on _____

5. My worst teacher was _____

   My worst subject was _____

6. I had   too much / too little   body hair (circle one)

7. What scared me the most about the opposite sex was _____

   What scared me most about the same sex was _____

8. My main source of information about sex was _____

9. I could tell my secrets to _____

10. The adult I trusted or who "understood" was _____

11. The secret I never told anyone was _____

12. My most disgusting habit was _____

13. My most embarrassing moment was _____

14. My most powerful moment was _____

15. I was different from everyone else because _____

16. The thing I wanted to change the most about myself was ____

    _____

17. I most wanted to be _____

18. One thing I've forgotten about those years is _____

19. One thing I'll never forget is _____

▲ ADULT-TEEN QUESTIONS FOR FACILITATORS

In preparation for working with youth, talk through the questions in Part I with co-leaders or other parents, co-workers or friends. Then try the exercises in Part II as a group.

Part I

1. What is one thing about teens that drives you up the wall? Or, think of a teenager you don't like: what is it about her/him you don't like?

2. Think of *any* way this person reminds you of how it was for you as a teenager, e.g., any ways you acted, anything you didn't like about yourself or someone else disapproved of in you. What is it about *you* that may make this kind of young person difficult to be with?

3. For a moment, interpret the teenager's characteristic or behavior as a survival mechanism for him or her; can you make a good justification for why he/she is acting that way?

4. When you were a teen, who was an adult who came through for you? What did they do? How could you tell they were on your side?

5. In your work with youth now, what kind of support could you use most from other adults around you? What might get in your way of asking for this support?

Part II

1. What is the hardest, or most fearful, or most embarrassing situation or remark you expect when you encounter teens in a classroom? What is the worst thing that could happen?

2. With other facilitators playing teens and adults, act out this scene, exaggerating everything, and do the most outrageously *wrong* thing you can think of to deal with the situation as a facilitator. Blow it completely and hilariously. Notice the feelings.

3. Process the feelings, and then brainstorm responses that turn this "problem" into a learning process for the whole class.

WORKING WITH TEENS
by Allan Creighton

As adults and youth who work with and support teenagers, we can use some help and direction in how to do this work well. Those of us who are adults are part of a group which, in fact and in their perception, has discriminated against and sometimes exercised power abusively over teens. It gets hard for us to think clearly about teenagers because we are ex-teenagers, with our own unresolved conflicts from those years. After all, adults exercised power abusively over us when we were young.

Teenagers and children have all been touched intimately by abuse and violence. If we define abuse as restricting, controlling, humiliating, or hurting another, it's clear that abuse is a daily experience for young people. We have a new word for it: adultism.

There are the obvious examples of adultism: physical and sexual abuse, "discipline," fights, the corporal "toughening up" process for boys and the instilling of fear in girls. But beyond this, there are emotional, verbal, financial, sexual, social, and political forms of abuse. Perhaps the most pervasive forms of this abuse are in our educational process itself, carried on in schools, families, religious and cultural institutions, and public media. This process, despite its best intentions, continually invalidates or trivializes young people's intelligence, denies access to important information they need (e.g., about birth control) and then faults them for not having it, subjects them to control or dependence arbitrarily, and denies them life resources—money, transportation, the chance to speak for and represent themselves, and so forth. Perhaps most crucially, it continually passes on our own beliefs as adults that there are limits to what people can do and to what the world will allow—in other words, we teach them our own hopelessness.

The still-pervasive teaching of male and female roles—that women are to be dependent victims and men abusive monsters—is a disaster for young people. In teenagers we find both powerful resistance to such teachings and, at the same time, internalizations of them. Teenagers both fight the roles and inhabit them; they learn to abuse one another and themselves.

How can we be allies of young people in these circumstances? The first thing to affirm is that we *are* allies. We care, and we are in a great position to be allies. All of us have memories of an adult or two that was there for us, and we all have some immediate information about what we can do. But more basically, just being an adult who cares and is willing to do something to express that care is a complete contradiction to the hurt that many adults do.

There is a lot more that we can do. The following suggestions are meant for those of us who work with teens in an educational setting, and talk about family, peer, and relationship violence.

Standing in a classroom talking to teens, we are participating in an adult-constructed institution which contributes to the power inequality between adults and teens, which is, in fact, a symbol of that inequality to many young people. Being aware of the power dynamics in this setting, as well as the barriers already set in place by the adult abuse teens experience outside this institution, is a prerequisite to being an effective ally. This also means being aware of the existence of other power differences, (e.g., racial and class inequalities) that may separate adult presenters from teenagers in the classroom. "Being aware" does not mean being paralyzed by or helpless about! It means having considered where our own confusions are about these differences, having a sense of where confusion and misinformation may exist for young people, and being prepared to talk about them, up front.

As adults, the best thing we can do with teens right from the start is to contradict directly, in our actions, the traditional adult behavior teens often encounter. For example, where they are traditionally denied information, we provide it, answering all questions and not faulting the asker for lacking the facts. No question is trivial. Similarly, teenagers and children hear in hundreds of ways that they are stupid or not smart enough. In contrast, we take as a starting point that they are doing everything they can, in the ways that are available to them, to live creative and nonabusive lives. We assume that the only blocks to their success are the abuses that happen and have happened to them.

Again, they have incorrect information, or misinformation, for example, about how boys and girls are supposed to act, or how they are "naturally" or biologically. This is in addition to the misinformation passed on to them by adults about race, class, sexual orientation, and so forth. They are not to be told they are wrong for believing these

Unity Photo: Alan Kondo ©1992

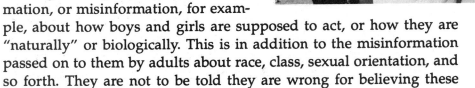

things, since it makes sense that you believe stereotypes about African-Americans or Jews or people with disabilities if the whole culture is at work teaching them to you. We can only correct such beliefs by keeping the discussion open and having teens work out answers with each other.

This work is in large part about making information—and thereby power—accessible. And it is at least in part about leaving room for some feelings about how one has been abused already. To carry on this work we must make what we say simple and direct, structured around a few basic goals. We can be clear and use real-life language. In particular, we can avoid the jargon we have all learned to use that distances us what we are saying (Hmmm... "distances us" is such jargon, isn't it?) Words like "perpetrator," "instigate," "continuum," and even "violence" can be walls to real experience.

This work is also about how we as adults can learn from young people and how they can teach us. By thinking about the traditional roles of young people, we immediately begin to think about the traditional roles of adults. About how much work we are supposed to do. About having to make our own way unaided in a world alive with violence, where power is unequally distributed by race, gender, class, age, and the rest. About having to know everything. About having the responsibility for the support, maintenance, physical and mental health, and safety, twenty-four hours a day, of other human beings (young people) *and* ourselves. We notice how we have all learned what consequences can follow from making mistakes. We get to think about the lies we have ingested from counselors, educators, and childcare experts—lies that say this should be easy, and if I find it hard there is something wrong with me—the chronic feeling all adults get that "I've been trying so hard, but it's not good enough."

Letting down the adult "guard" we've learned by sharing power with young people in the classroom is a refreshing relief from this oppressive role. By turning to them to find out from them, as experts, what they think and what their lives are like now, we lighten this load. Giving up the role of being the omniscient teacher with all the answers gives us a chance to be learners ourselves.

Cultures across the world have always turned to young people for inspiration. Their hope that the world can be different, their outright insistence on justice and fair treatment (sometimes mislabeled "rebelliousness"), their insight and irreverence are essential to our own freedom. Acknowledging this to ourselves is a crucial step forward in this work.

Adults do not routinely show respect to teens or treat teenagers as having equal rights. Here again we can turn the situation around by being personal, direct, speaking for ourselves and from our own experiences, with honesty and respect. Informally. And with humor.

Part of the misinformation teenagers may carry is about themselves, and it is always appropriate for us to interrupt it. A boy who has learned that men are, on basic levels, monsters, needs adults who clearly believe that men have learned violence but are not naturally abusive. This boy will also benefit from being around adults who support the many ways men resist abuse, including crying when they are hurt, walking away from fights, seeking nontraditional careers, and fighting for the rights of women and children. A girl who has learned that women survive based upon how they look and how they relate to men needs an adult ally who supports her efforts to move beyond these limited conceptions.

Another part of the disaster of adultism is the teaching of all the other oppressions to young people—especially those of race, class, and sexual orientation. Here too, our supportive interruptions are crucial (and, of course, not easy to make). A racist or homophobic remark left in place hurts everyone, including the utterer. It lowers the teen community's hopes that these oppressions can be overcome and eliminated from the world. It passes on, directly, the abuse that keeps teens separated from each other in the first place.

Teens do form a community; they have learned what they have learned together and they have experienced control by adults as a class. Our calling on them to resist abuse as a community is a genuine act of alliance. It means supporting them in recognizing their strengths and the ways they have resisted abuse. Further, it means expecting them to be powerful and to handle their problems by reaching out to each other, with our help and confidence backing them up.

Finally, we do this work for ourselves and to keep alive our own hope for a nonabusive world. We should not hunt for or expect gratitude from teenagers. We can just enjoy being with teens, teaching and learning together. We do good work and can get our support for it elsewhere, by finding other adults to talk with, especially when our hopelessness about things, or our own unresolved teen issues, creep back in. We must support each other, make loads of mistakes, fix them, and get on with our work.

ADULTS AS ALLIES OF TEENS
adapted from Paul Kivel and the Oakland Men's Project

The following general guidelines apply to adults who work with teens. To be able to follow them, adults must be able to support each other and get help from each other when this work gets hard. Guideline number one is: we as adults back each other up and take time with each other.

After that,

Teens need adults to . . .

▲ listen

▲ model strength, openness, respect, trust, and cooperation

▲ encourage and support the same in teens

▲ provide information

▲ respect the intelligence of everyone at all times

▲ value teens' fears and problems as genuine

▲ help each person identify personal issues and solutions

▲ provide a clear, understandable conceptual framework to aid in personal problem-solving

▲ provide lots of options and encourage the creation of new options

▲ not try to force change on anyone

▲ prevent trashing—adult to teen, teen to adult, and teen to teen

▲ prevent rudeness, judging (especially judgments about appearance), lecturing, attitudes of disrespect, or the attitude that one is "incorrect" or blameworthy for what she/he believes at the present time

▲ recognize that small steps and activities are important and need to be encouraged

▲ acknowledge that people are doing the best they can given the information they possess and the thinking they have been allowed to do

▲ not rescue young people; at the same time, be prepared with resources should they be needed and requested

▲ facilitate teens' self-consciousness as a group: foster their chances to share information with one another, respect one another, and experience their power as a group

▲ refer the group back to its own resources

- emphasize local community information, services, and networks

- bring out the common features of teens' experience of hurt, resistance to hurt, and power

- facilitate the breaking down of family and group insularity that prevent community intervention in abusive situations

- talk from the heart

And, more generally, **teens need adults to . . .**

- understand the systematic mistreatment that young people receive in this adult-defined world and correct that mistreatment

- welcome and celebrate making mistakes and be willing to risk and learn

- support teens being 100% powerful

- and lastly, in the face of all of the above and with all of our concerns about violence and abuse, teens need adults to *lighten up!*

THE BASIC AGREEMENTS

Throughout the manual we refer to the following basic agreements we make with participants at the outset of any class or support group, in order to build trust, honor, respect, and closeness among us in the group. With them, we establish the safety crucial for healing, liberation, and justice. We recommend you establish commitments like these in work you do with youth. Sometimes youths will say they wish that they had these agreements at home, in their family. *These agreements actually model the healthy, nonviolent relationships we are trying to achieve.*

1. Confidentiality

Each person agrees to keep what comes up in the group confidential, unless it is dangerous to do so—that is, unless a situation described in the group really requires us to get some outside help. This means that I don't repeat what someone else says in the group outside the group without getting permission from that person. It also means that I don't talk to that person outside the group about what they said in the group without getting their permission. And if they say "No," it means no.

2. Amnesty

As a companion to confidentiality, everyone agrees not to treat others differently, blame them, or hold or use what they say in the group against them after the group ends. This is particularly crucial where members have relationships outside the group, such as parent/child, boss/worker, teacher/student, boyfriend/girlfriend.

3. Put-ups, not put-downs

Everyone agrees not to put down, make fun of, minimize, or attack other people in the group—or themselves. (Putting myself down happens, for example, when I begin my statements by saying things like "Well, this probably isn't important, but . . . " or "This may sound stupid, but . . . .")

4. Right to pass

Each person has the right not to talk in the group when they don't want to.

5. No cross-talk, no piggy-backing

Each person has a chance to say what they want without having it debated, denied, or attacked, *or* agreed with or supported. The statement gets to stand on its own, without being taken over by someone else.

6. Feelings

Everyone in the group will experience feelings of hurt, sadness, boredom, or anger at sometime. That expression of feeling is part of the healing process. Each person agrees to respect and allow expression of those feelings, *including her or his own.*

7. Respect/listening

Each person agrees to listen to others in the group and to expect that the group will listen to them. This also means that one person talks at a time.

8. I-statements

People agree to speak for themselves and their own experiences when talking and not to speak for others unless asked to. This means using the word "I" in place of the words "you," "we," or "they." This is a *very* difficult agreement to keep, but a crucial one. It helps us to speak about what is true for us and keep close to how each of us feels. Much of what we have to unlearn, after all, is misinformation about "them," "you," or "us."

9. Try on the process

Everyone agrees to try on the process. No one is required to agree with it or accept it . . . just to try it on.

10. Take care of and enjoy yourself

Everyone agrees as much as possible to take charge of their own needs (taking stretch and bathroom breaks, making themselves physically comfortable, asking for help when they need it, and so forth). This includes enjoying and having fun during the process.

We always finish with:

11. Other agreements

Ask members of the group to add any other agreements they want the group to commit to in order to increase their safety in the group.

Additional agreements can be made for particular groups, for example, about no drug or alcohol use, about punctuality, etc. (See "Support Group Agreements," pages 112–113.) For extended workshops (overnights or weekends) we might add an agreement about no sexual contact between group members, both to build safety and to encourage participants (and facilitators) to notice what feelings might be behind the urge for sexual contact.

Section 2

Liberation Theory and Practice

Unity Photo: Michael Lichter ©1992

This section describes the philosophy underlying our work with young people to stop family and relationship violence. "It's About Power" analyzes social power relations in the United States through a series of exercises which demonstrate how power differences affect us, how they create conditions conducive to violence, and how we can establish "alliances" to become more powerful.

The remaining articles apply the theory presented in "It's About Power" to the specific power imbalances of sexism, racism, anti-Semitism, heterosexism, classism, and "adultism" (the power imbalance of adults over young people). We have highlighted these particular issues because of their immediate relevance to young people. The theory can easily be extended to other social inequalities.

This section also includes many of the key exercises we use in workshops. These will be referred to throughout the book. In a book, as in a classroom, theory is hard to digest and takes time. Use this section as a reference to read around in and refer back to as you use the curricula and agendas that follow.

IT'S ABOUT POWER
by Allan Creighton and Paul Kivel

In the classroom with young people, and in workshops among adults, there are differences—differences in gender, racial and ethnic heritage, age, physical ability, economic class, sexual orientation, and many others. Some differences are visible, some we look for automatically, some we may pretend not to see. But what is true about these differences is that they are used to separate people along lines of power. This power takes the form of access to resources, work, housing, education, physical security, protection by law, and representation in government. And while some groups are socially sanctioned to be powerful, they are permitted to have this power at the expense of other groups, whose access to resources is correspondingly limited or denied.

The social perspective from which Battered Women's Alternatives and the Oakland Men's Project operate is that the primary root of violence in the United States is the systematic, institutionalized, and day-to-day imbalance of power. What this means to those social groups that do not have equal power—women, children, people of color, workers, and the rest—is that they have less control over their lives and are targets of physical and sexual violence, discrimination, harassment, and poverty at home, in the workplace, and in the wider community.

This pattern of power imbalance is continually renewed through the training of each generation of young people. When children in this country learn misinformation about groups of people different than themselves through lies, jokes, stereotypes, rewritten history, and biased research, they are being trained to justify, enforce, and continue the power differences.

And since all social inequalities reinforce one another, it becomes clear that violence against women and children will not be stopped unless violence against people of color, gays, lesbians, Jews, people with disabilities, working-class people, elders, and the rest is also eliminated. Moreover, we cannot expect to support young people in "unlearning" the lies of sexism unless we are prepared to assist them and ourselves in unlearning the other "isms."

We need to say something about language as we begin to explore issues of power more closely, because language itself is an instrument of power and is often used to control others. Throughout this book we use the terms "sexism," "racism," "anti-Semitism," "heterosexism," and "adultism" as terms describing different oppressions, conscious that although they are in common usage, they are more or less inadequate and even misleading. "Anti-Semitism" as a synonym for the oppression of Jews hides the fact that there are non-Jewish Semitic (Arab) people who are oppressed in ways different from Jews. "Adultism" as a term for the oppression of young people defines the oppression in terms of the oppressor, not the victim. "Heterosexism" is slightly less clumsy than "the oppression of gays, lesbians, and bisexuals," but usually only means heterosexual prejudice, not the full-blown oppression. Names for nonpower groups are always problematic, since they are almost always picked by power groups. Take "teen" for example, a word which adults often use to trivialize, judge, or diminish young people. Part of all unlearning is continuing to question our terminology.

We explore the power differences described above through the following exercises, focussing on the key concepts of:

power and nonpower groups

oppression

internalized oppression

alliance building

▲ Power Shuffle
by Harrison Simms

Everyone stands and gathers at one end of the room, after moving desks, chairs, etc. aside. The facilitator stands to the front and side of the group. The facilitator states that they will be giving the group a series of instructions. Participants are asked to follow the instructions silently, paying attention to who is with them and who is separated from them, and to feelings that come up while performing this exercise.

The facilitator states that people do not have to identify themselves as members of a group that is called out if they don't wish to, but should notice any feelings that come up about not identifying themselves. If anyone is unsure about which group they belong to, they are to decide themselves where it makes sense for them to go.

With each instruction, the facilitator asks certain people to move across the room from the full group, turn, and look back. The two groups then stand still for a few seconds, observing each other and their own feelings. Then the facilitator brings them together again for the next "shuffle."

For each category, the facilitator says: "Please step to the other side of the room if you are . . . [the category]. [Pause.] Notice who's standing with you. Notice who's not. [Pause.] Notice how you feel. [Pause.] Come back together."

Phrases in parenthesis in this exercise are alternative statements we use, depending on the composition of the group.

The exercise:

Please step to the other side of the room if

1. You are a woman

2. You are Asian, East-Asian/Indian, or Pacific Islander

3. You are Latino/a, Chicano/a, or mestizo/a

4. You are of Arabian descent

5. You are Native American Indian, or at least one of your parents or grandparents is full-blooded Native American Indian

6. You are African-American or black, or of African descent

7. You are of multi-heritage, and at least one of your parents or grandparents is a person of color

8. You are of Jewish heritage

9. You are 45 or over

10. You are 24 (*or:* under 18)

11. You were raised poor

12. You were raised by a single parent or currently are a single parent

13. Your parent/s or the people who raised you were or are working-class and did manual labor, skilled or unskilled work, or pink-collar clerical or service work to make a living

14. You were raised in an isolated or farming community

15. Neither of your parents, or the people who raised you, attended college (*or:* received a college degree)

16. You were raised Catholic

17. You have a visible or hidden physical disability or impairment

18. You have ever been dangerously or continually sick

19. You are an immigrant to this country

20. Your native language is other than English

21. You come from a family where alcohol or drugs were/are a problem

22. You were raised in or are now part of a religious community that is other than Christian

23. You are lesbian, gay, or bisexual (always decide whether it is safe enough to call out this category and don't be overcautious; if no one walks across, you can point out the lack of safety in the group later)

24. Someone in your family or a close friend is gay/lesbian/bisexual

25. You are a nonmanagement worker and/or do not supervise anyone on your job

26. You are now or ever have been unemployed, not by choice

27. You are a veteran

28. You or a member of your family has ever been labeled mentally ill or crazy

29. You or a member of your family have ever been incarcerated or been in the juvenile justice system

30. You were ever publicly labeled fat, whether or not you ever *felt* fat

31. You have ever been a child, whether you felt you were allowed to be one or not (*or:* if you as a child ever had an adult's needs put ahead of yours)

Other categories may be added as appropriate, and some of these can be deleted depending upon the composition of the group, the issues to be covered, and the amount of time available.

The facilitator then has participants walk to the center of the room and, for a few moments, mingle silently, making eye contact and acknowledging each other as people present together in this group. Then participants pair up to describe the feelings they had while doing this exercise. Finally, the group is brought back together and people are asked to share responses to the exercise.

▲ Power Chart

The Power Chart exercise allows participants to identify for themselves some of the inequities of power that exist in the United States.

The exercise is begun with a blank chart. The group is asked to provide examples of social groups in the United States that have power and their counterparts that are denied power. The result of this exercise should look something like the chart shown below. If any key groups are missing, the facilitators can add them.

Power	Nonpower
adult	youth
men	women
white	people of color
rich	poor
adult	elder
heterosexual	lesbian/gay/bisexual
people without disabilities	people with disabilities
"normal"	"crazy"
boss	worker
Gentile	Jew
"normal"	"fat"
teacher	student

There are a number of things we notice immediately about this chart and the group can discuss these issues together.

Power/nonpower

We describe the difference between the two sides of the chart by noting that the right side consists of "nonpower" groups, the left of "power" groups. In each category, one group has more power than the other group. This does not mean that "nonpower" groups are intrinsically powerless, it means that society creates conditions that give them less power than the corresponding groups on the left. Looking at this chart, we can see that another major consequence of this power difference is that nonpower groups are targeted for violence—in the narrowest and widest senses of that term—by the corresponding power groups. The group can discuss these issues: for example, what violence is done to children by adults? To people of color by white people? To women by men?

The violence is institutionalized

Nonpower groups undergo systematic, routine, day-to-day discrimination and mistreatment, in forms as basic as access to jobs, food, and housing. As members of nonpower groups, we frequently experience this violence *as* individuals, and often experience it *from* individuals, but it has its source in already existing institutional inequality. The institutions of family, education, work, business, religion, housing, law, and government in which we are raised sustain this inequality. Inequality is made to look "normal," or it is made invisible or denied. But it is precisely because inequality is institutionalized that the mistreatment of nonpower groups is so complete.

There is no reverse "ism"

Since the institutional imbalance is in one direction—power over nonpower—it is counterproductive to use concepts like "reverse racism," "reverse sexism," and so forth. Individuals in the nonpower group can stereotype or have prejudices about people in the power

group. They can act aggressively toward them. But the power imbalance nonetheless targets nonpower groups—nonpower groups do not have the social power and command of resources to limit the powerful or to protect themselves from system-wide violence.

Our differences do not cause the power imbalance

This cannot be emphasized too strongly: our differences do not cause the institutional power imbalances; they are used to justify already existing imbalances. People do not earn mistreatment because they are Latino, or women, or have disabilities. There is nothing natural or biological about these differences that causes oppression. Rather, the imbalance of power is there first, and we are all exposed to it as children, learning lies about target groups long before we actually meet any of these individuals.

The stereotypes are taught to us as a means of justifying the imbalance. For example, "African-Americans are mentally inferior, so they are better suited for menial jobs," or "Women are natural nurturers, so they should do all the housework and childcare." These

Unity Photo: Cynthia Mata-Flores ©1992

lies enable a society to justify forcing these groups to take care of its most difficult and exhausting work and to rationalize discrimination and unequal pay for comparable work.

We live on both sides

What do you notice about where you live on this chart?

The first thing to see is that each of us has places on both sides. Each of us knows what it is like to be in a position of power and what it's like to have someone have power over us. Each of us, as a member of a nonpower group, has experienced mistreatment and learned lies about ourself. Each of us, as a member of a power group, has learned lies about the nonpower group and about ourself as a power group member. We have been placed in a position of relative privilege over the nonpower group members, and we have been socially sanctioned to discriminate against them.

You may also notice that it is possible to experience being on both sides of some categories. For example, all of us have been or are children, all of us are or will become adults, many of us are or will become elders.

THE CYCLE OF VIOLENCE

We all learn in this society that power means "power over," and that if we are targeted for violence in one area, the easiest way to deal with it is to find a place where we have power over someone else and pass the pain on to them. If your boss leans on you at work, or if your dad yelled at and hit you as a child, then you are permitted to take it out on someone younger than you. Or on a woman if you are a man, on a person of color if you are white, on a gay person if you are heterosexual.

The "learning" process and emotional pain

We all start out in a nonpower group: children. Training in power differences is passed on to us by people whom we love and trust, at a time when it is difficult to evaluate what we are taught. Every instance of this passing on is painful and counts as violence. Where the "training" involves physical or sexual abuse, it is obviously violence, obviously producing injury and physical pain. But there is another effect of the conditioning process that has potentially more damaging long-term consequences: *emotional* pain. Emotional pain is inner suffering and distress, often suppressed, often unconscious, which influences how we negotiate our relationships as we grow up. Based on hurtful experience, our distress falsifies our sense of the world and inhibits us from thinking creatively about the present and future.

Emotional pain ranges across an entire spectrum of feelings, from lowered self-worth to confusion about the world, from hopelessness about being able to survive and prosper to inexplicable panic, from slow-burning anger to the absence of any feelings whatever. What these feelings have in common is that they keep the "learning" in place, unchallenged. As a result, any *unlearning* requires emotional safety—space and time to notice and express the feelings in order to move beyond them.

It is awful to be targeted for abuse; it is awful to learn that your group targets others for abuse. Young people resist as best they can. But the training is thorough, and a final effect of the process is that we learn to accept mistreatment as "normal" and "natural" while forgetting the painful conditions under which we had misinformation imposed upon us. "It wasn't so bad . . . it's just part of growing up . . . nothing bad happened to me."

Finally, in understanding and beginning to dismantle this unjust system, we use three essential concepts.

1. Oppression

Pick an issue on which you are in the nonpower group, and notice how people on your side of the line are mistreated by people on the other side. Think of physical, emotional, mental, verbal, economic, social, and political forms of this mistreatment. We call this violence *oppression*. Let's look at three of the categories as examples:

Power	Nonpower	Oppression
adult	youth	hitting, sexual assault, neglect, exploitation, verbal abuse, withheld rights and choices
men	women	rape, battering, harassment, economic discrimination, poverty, poor healthcare
white	people of color	physical assault, segregation, economic discrimination, poor healthcare, police brutality, withheld education, poverty, extermination of native peoples

Notice that many of the same hurts are done to people all up and down the nonpower side.

2. Internalized oppression

Oppression that goes on long enough is internalized. If we grow up continually being taught lies about who we are, we come to believe them. Think about the same nonpower group you picked in #1. What are you sometimes afraid is true about what they say regarding people in your group (even if you "know" rationally that it's not true)? Let's use the same three categories as examples.

Power	Nonpower	Internalized Oppression
adult	youth	"kids are losers" "they deserve what they get" "kids are so immature" "some kids are just bad" "I'm not old enough" "I don't have anything important to say"
men	women	"some women are flighty" "some women will use sex to get what they want" "maybe women are too emotional"
white	people of color	"some of my people really are lazy" "if they *really* wanted to, they could succeed" "some of them *are* stupid" "they'll never amount to anything"

Internalized oppression is as pervasive as oppression, teaching members of a nonpower group to attack, give up on, and separate themselves from each other, as well as to attack, compete with, and separate themselves from other nonpower groups. Even worse, it trains each person to isolate and blame ourself and each other.

▲ Nonpower visualization (part 1)

Pick a category on the nonpower side of the chart that you belong to. (If on this particular chart you are only on the power side, use your previous experience of being a youth.)

Close your eyes and visualize a personal experience you have had of being hurt, abused, or discriminated against by a person or people from the corresponding group on the power side of the chart. (For example, if you picked "woman" as your category, think of an experience of being hurt by a man or men.)

Notice how it feels.

Think of a way that you have internalized that violence by blaming yourself or questioning what you did or how you responded.

Open your eyes and describe how it feels to remember that experience.

Imagining all the people in the room as your best friends, what could you most use from the rest of the class to deal with or recover from the personal experience you just recalled. (This is a group sharing—list answers on the board.)

3. Alliance

We can fight back against both external oppression and internalized oppression by being clear first, that they exist and affect us, and second, that we will not accept either one.

For the nonpower group

In particular, this means being an ally to people in your own nonpower group. When women come together, when African-American people organize, when workers unite, they break down the isolation and blame of internalized oppression and begin to resist oppression directly. When these groups in turn link their struggle with other groups up and down the nonpower side, their strength is increased exponentially.

Ultimately, this struggle means holding the people directly across the line on the power side accountable for being complete allies for you and your group. This means expecting that mistreatment is not inevitable and can be ended. It means refusing to accept limitations on your power, remembering all the ways you and the people in your group have resisted mistreatment, and expecting that power group people do not "naturally" engage in mistreatment but want, more than anything, for it to end.

▲ Nonpower visualization (part 2)

Using the nonpower group you used in Part 1 of this exercise, visualize how your group has come together historically to resist violence and gain power? How have you successfully resisted the oppression and internalized oppression affecting your group?

What do you and people in your group demand, require, and expect from people across the line from you, as total allies of yours? Accepting anything less than complete alliance from them is a way of giving up on your power to accept no limits, to be unlimited. (In a workshop the facilitator might list the group's responses on the board.)

For the power group

Each of us in our power roles agrees to be an ally to nonpower groups, refusing to accept misinformation about and mistreatment of them, and *always* intervening. This means remembering all the ways that we, as members of our power groups, have resisted learning about mistreatment, taking pride in *our* people, finding and celebrating all the ways they resisted learning the oppressor role, and refusing to accept that they want mistreatment to continue. It means refusing to give in to guilt or defensiveness, and instead believing in our own good will—taking steps, making mistakes, fixing them, and going on to be close and full allies for people across the line.

Pick a power group that you are a member of and answer the following questions:

What are you unreservedly proud of about your people?

What are ways you and your people have resisted learning and passing on oppression?

What is your next step in being a proud ally to people across the line?

These concepts are integral to our work with young people. That work is liberation, and liberation only works when all of us choose to be free, to break out of the cycle of oppression and internalized oppression, and to be allies for each other's freedom. It is exciting, creative, and joyous work. Let's get on with it.

TALKING ABOUT SEXISM AND SEXIST VIOLENCE: WORKING ASSUMPTIONS
by Allan Creighton

Adapted from Erica Sherover-Marcuse, "Towards a Perspective on Unlearning Racism"

Acts of violence against women, such as rape, battering, and sexual harassment, are rooted in sexism—the systematic mistreatment of women by men. It is systematic both because it extends throughout the society, taking physical, emotional, political, social, and economic forms, and because it affects every one of us—man, woman, and child.

Sexism is the system of attitudes, assumptions, actions, and institutions which makes women vulnerable to violence and subject to discrimination and disrespect. It is intensified and compounded by other systematic imbalances of power among people differentiated by class, age, race, sexual orientation, and physical and mental ability.

Part of the task of working actively to break down institutionalized sexism is to unlearn sexist attitudes and beliefs. They get in the way of our working together to create a society where men and women have equal power.

Below are 14 working assumptions on unlearning sexism and combating the sexual violence that is its expression. They "work" to the extent that they enable men and women proudly and happily to undertake the process of attitude change. (Along with the assumptions there are exercises and explanations we use in the classroom.)

Assumption 1

The systematic abuse of women isolates and divides us from each other. This process is a hurt to all of us. It dulls our sense of what is possible, conditions us to accept injustice, leads us to rationalize unacceptable human suffering, and keeps us from our strength in human community. We learn, simply, to give up on one another.

Assumption 2

Sexism is not biological or natural. No human being is born a male chauvinist, a darling housewife, or a rapist—anatomy is not destiny, boys need not be boys. Physical differences between human beings are not the cause of sexism; they are used as an excuse for sexism.

In particular, male/female roles are socially constructed. They are taught to us as children and enforced by teasing, harassment, threats, and abuse. The very first question asked about us is "Is it a boy or a girl?" Completely different treatments await us based upon the answer. Anatomical difference is used to justify already established male/female stereotypes—misinformation—that in turn justify already existing mistreatment. For example, all of us have the capacity to care for and nurture others, but men are specifically taught that these are "feminine," motherly characteristics. They learn on the playground and in the living room to devalue these traits in women, other men, and themselves—indeed, to bond with other men by ridiculing "feminine" behavior. (All those jokes.) Caring and nurturing are *human* traits. But the stereotypes can be used magically to justify keeping women out of the boardroom and men out of (minimum-wage or no-wage) childcare.

Another deadly function of these roles is heterosexism. Discrimination against gays, lesbians, and bisexuals is first learned by boys when they are taught that their major job in life is to "have" a woman and be tough and aggressive with other men—or else. Girls are pushed toward the catching, caring for, and maintenance of men as their job—or else. Intimate relations of any kind are and ought to be possible between members of the same sex, but sexism teaches boys and girls to be terrified of such intimacy. Calling someone a "fag" in the right tone of voice can start a fight in almost any high school in this country. That's terror.

But finally the roles are about violence itself. One entire group of human beings is raised to act out and enforce the power structures we see in the power chart—to be the soldiers and policemen, the designated users of violence, of the world. There is no way to calculate the damage done to men, the fear and rage they carry, or the devastation they enact because of this training. The corresponding non-power group is raised to care for the first group under threat of that violence—each woman has to live every day on a double track, doing what she normally does *and* making decisions consciously or subconsciously about physical safety at the bus stop, on the streets, at the office, on campus, at the job site, at the clinic, on the jogging trail, and in the bedroom. And in the end, regardless of the preparation, women undergo violence anyway, most often within the most intimate relationships, in unprecedented numbers and with immeasurable ferocity, leaving an unlimited legacy of fear.

Unity Photo: Francisco Garcia ©1992

Assumption 3

No young person acquires misinformation voluntarily. Sexist attitudes and beliefs are a mixture of lies and ignorance which has to be imposed upon young people through a painful process of social training. Boys have to be pushed and pressured for years to measure up; girls have to be curbed and trained for years to submit. We have to be taught to hate and fear. All of this training counts as violence against young people, and it takes different forms for boys and for girls.

Here is a two-part stand-up exercise we use in high school classrooms as well as in adult workshops, to show the abusive content of being taught to act like a man or act like a lady. The facilitator may delete some statements, especially in the classroom, because of the limited safety of disclosure.

▲ Men stand-up

All men in the room are instructed to stand at each of the following statements that applies to them, notice who else is standing, and notice their feelings. Then they sit, and the next statement is read. All have the right to pass, but are asked to notice their feelings if they do.

The exercise:

Please stand up silently if

1. You have ever worried you were not tough enough

2. You have ever exercised to make yourself tougher

3. You were ever told not to cry

4. You were ever hit to make you stop crying

5. You have ever been called a wimp, queer, or fag

6. You have ever been told to act like a man

7. You have ever been hit by an older man

8. You have ever been forced to fight, or were in a fight because you felt you had to prove you were a man

9. You ever saw an adult man you looked up to or respected hit or emotionally brutalize a woman

10. You have ever been physically injured by another person

11. You have ever been injured on a job

12. You have ever been physically injured and hid the pain, or kept it to yourself

13. You were ever sexually touched in a way you didn't like by an older person

14. You ever stopped yourself from showing affection, hugging, or touching another man because of how it might look

15. You have ever been arrested or done time in jail or prison

16. You have ever been (or plan to be) in the military or are a vet

17. You ever got so mad that, while driving, you drove fast or lost control of the car

18. You ever drank or took other drugs to cover your feelings or hide pain

19. You ever felt like blowing yourself away

20. You were ever molested as a child or young person

21. You ever hurt another person physically

22. You ever hurt another person sexually, or were sexual with another person when they didn't want to be

At the close of the exercise, the group processes their feelings about the experience.

▲ Women stand-up

All women in the room are asked to stand at each of the following statements that applies to them, notice who else is standing, and notice their feelings. Then they sit, and the next statement is read. All have the right to pass, but are asked to notice their feelings if they do. This exercise is not safe for women to do if there are few women compared to the number of men, or if there has not already been some discussion of gender roles and violence. This is an excellent exercise for an all-women support or discussion group.

The exercise:

Please stand up silently if

1. You have ever worn makeup, shaved your legs or underarms, or worn nylons

2. You've ever worn uncomfortable, restrictive clothing—heels, a girdle, clothes that felt too tight or too revealing

3. You have ever been afraid you were not pretty enough

4. You ever felt you were not feminine enough

5. You ever changed your diet or exercised to change your body size, or body shape, or weight

6. You ever felt less important than a man

7. You ever pretended to be less intelligent than you are to protect a man's ego

8. You were afraid to speak or felt ignored because the men were doing all the talking

9. You ever felt limited in what careers were open to you

10. You ever earned less than a man for doing equal work

11. You were ever sexually pressured by a man in your workplace or at school

12. You were ever yelled at, commented upon, whistled at, touched, or harassed by a man in a public place

13. You were ever lied to by a man so he could get something he wanted

14. You have ever been called a bitch, a cunt, a slut, or a whore

15. You ever limited your activity or changed your plans to go somewhere out of fear for your physical safety

16. You routinely or daily make plans for or limit your activity because of fear for your physical safety

17. You ever stopped yourself from hugging, kissing, or holding hands with another woman for fear you might be called a lesbian

18. You were ever expected to take full responsibility for birth control

19. You have ever been pregnant when you didn't want to be

20. You ever had an abortion

21. You have ever been prescribed medication to control your emotions or spent time in counseling or in a mental institution because you were "too" emotional

22. You have ever been afraid of a man's anger

23. You have ever said "Yes" to a man because you were afraid to say "No"

24. You have ever been pressured to have sex with a man or had sex when you really didn't want to

25. You have ever been hit by a man

26. You have ever been raped by a man

27. You have ever been molested

To close the exercise, the group processes their feelings about the experience.

When we look at these physical and sexual correlates of sex-role "training," it becomes immediately clear how devastating the training process is, whether the events mentioned happen to us or we witness them happening to someone else.

Assumption 4

Lies and misinformation are harmful to all women and men. Having attitudes and beliefs which are sexist is like having a clamp on one's mind—it distorts one's perceptions of reality. Some examples are the beliefs that some women ask to be raped, or that black men are rapists. Lies like these obviously (and historically) function to justify violence by blaming the victims.

Assumption 5

No one believes lies voluntarily. People retain sexist attitudes and beliefs because it is the only information they have, because it is the best thinking they have been able to do at the time, and because no one has been able to help them out of this misinformation.

Assumption 6

People will change their minds about deeply held convictions when: (a) a new position is presented in a way that makes sense to them; (b) they trust the person who is presenting this new position; and (c) they are not being blamed for having believed misinformation.

Assumption 7

People hurt others because they have themselves been hurt. In this society, we have all experienced systematic mistreatment as young people, often through physical violence (in "discipline" or outright abuse) but also through the invalidation of our intelligence ("girls are stupid"), the disregard of our feelings ("act like a man"), and the discounting of our abilities ("you're only a kid").

Because of these experiences, we tend both to internalize this mistreatment by accepting it as the way things are, and to externalize it by mistreating others. Externalized mistreatment may be directly sexist, for example, in sexual harassment on the street, or it may be indirect, as when a man, feeling guilty or blamed, trashes other men for their behavior or accuses women of "reverse sexism."

(As we mentioned earlier, because sexism is systematic mistreatment, "reverse sexism" is a contradiction in terms. Of course individual women may mistreat individual men, but there is no systematic mistreatment of men by women. A man charging reverse sexism is, among other things, attempting to separate himself from his role as a member of the class which *does* systematically mistreat. He may also be trying, unfortunately through sexist means, to talk about how hard it is to be a man—how the training and expectations that go along with being a man are hurtful to men as well as women, even with the so-called payoff of having privilege over women.)

It makes sense that boys, constantly monitored by adults, carefully watch other boys to detect "unmasculine" traits; that girls, constantly graded by appearance, learn to compete with one another for men's attention. Part of the process of unlearning sexism involves becoming aware of how this painful cycle of mistreatment is kept alive in day-to-day encounters and interactions.

Assumption 8

As young people, we have witnessed despair and cynicism in adults around us and have often been made to feel powerless in the face of injustice. Rape and battering continue in part because people feel powerless to do anything about them.

Assumption 9

Sometimes we have failed to act, or haven't achieved as much as we wanted to, in the struggle against sexism. Unlearning sexism also involves understanding the difficulties we have had and learning how to overcome them without blaming ourselves.

Assumption 10

The situation is not hopeless. People can grow and change; the world as it stands is not built in stone. Everywhere, women actively fight violence and inequality—they are not "helpless" but are and can be strong leaders. And everywhere there are men who do not voluntarily approve of or engage in disrespect, discrimination, or abuse, and who do stop their own and other men's violence. Men can take responsibility for male violence; they are natural allies for women. Women can and do support and love one another and accept alliances with men. Men do achieve long-lasting intimate relationships with other men based on love and not oppression of women. Sexism can be examined, analyzed, fought against, and unlearned.

Assumption 11

There are many different ways to be male and female and many different kinds of personal and collective relationships between men and women. Misinformation we have learned about our own gender is often the flip side of misinformation about the others. A man who learns that men are naturally dominating, tough, and emotionless represents the flip side of a woman taught to believe all women must be nurturing, irrational, and passive.

A crucial part of unlearning sexism is the reclaiming of some truths about one's own sex. One truth is that both women and men can and have acted powerfully outside and in spite of the gender role training and the violence they have experienced. Reclaiming the truth about our struggles and victories enables us to take justified pride in our real histories of being men and women.

Assumption 12

We cannot make permanent change acting from guilt or hopelessness. We each come from personal heritages and traditions which have a history of resistance to sexism (and other types of socialization), and every person has their own individual history of resistance. When we recall and celebrate that resistance, we contradict the lies of sexism. When people act from a sense of informed pride and joy in themselves and their own traditions, they will be more effective in all struggles for justice.

Assumption 13

Men who speak out against sexism contradict the beliefs that men are inevitably abusive to women, that men will never change, and that they cannot be trusted by women. As such men, we can expect that when we make mistakes, say the wrong thing, or act on our own sexism inadvertently, women will be angry at us. Having invited their trust, we will in our actions have supported the distressing, hopeless feeling that men will always be the same, and we will have hurt them directly with sexism. To be a true ally to women is to hear the anger and understand its source in feelings of hopelessness and experiences of mistreatment; to listen, take criticism, make changes, and in general make it clear that we are delighted to do so. We do not do this work as just another way to get women's support or approval or gratitude or trust.

Other men may be angered when we speak out, breaking the chain of collusion. They may feel deserted or unfairly blamed, or they may see us as hypocritical. To contradict men's learned cynicism, it is crucial not to fault or attack men for their misinformation. By caring for and accepting them, while confronting their beliefs and attitudes, we demonstrate the potential for strong and loving alliances against injustice among men.

Assumption 14

Lies about gender reinforce and reflect social inequality. They do not cause it, but are caused by it. They serve to justify or cover up the domination of many women and men by a few men, because they give all men limited rights to dominate.

The full unlearning of sexism involves the active undoing of gender-wide inequality. Unlearning or changing an attitude is not enough; understanding sexism is not enough. This is something we act upon. The point of understanding the world is to change it.

RACISM
by Paul Kivel and Allan Creighton

Oppression

Racism is the systematic, institutionalized mistreatment of one group by another when the groups are differentiated by perceived or imputed skin color. In the United States, the group benefiting most from power is clearly white people, just as in much of the world the white-dominated economy has power. The groups targeted for mistreatment here are people of Arabic, Asian, Pacific Islander, African-American, Latin American, and Native American descent, and people of mixed heritage. In this system, whites have the economic,

Unity Photo: Michael Lichter ©1992

physical, emotional, legal, and political power to exploit, control, or violate people of color. It doesn't matter that many, even most white people do not consciously or actively seek such power; simply by being white they enjoy material advantages and privileges unknown to people of color.

Again, many white people claim to have experienced mistreatment or prejudice from people of color. Sometimes this claim is used to justify stereotyping and mistreatment of people of color. But because racism is institutional, the power is always on the side of the institutions, which favor white people. And these institutions have taught white people the stereotypes long before they experienced any mistreatment or prejudice from people of color. Anyone from any group can have personal attitudes of prejudice towards others. But racism is not about prejudice—it is about power. And in American society, only white people have the power to enforce systematic, institutionalized racism.

Human beings are members of the same species. There are relatively few biological differences between any racial groups. But we are born into a society in which racial power imbalances are already established. It is a cycle: established inequalities are enforced by institutions, which in turn teach us that the power imbalance is natural and appropriate. The exploitation of one group by another is justified by statements about the inferiority of that group; they are said to be less than human in various ways.

Some of the direct results of racism are:

▲ shorter life spans of people of color

▲ higher infant mortality and poorer healthcare in general

▲ less access to jobs, lower wages, more dangerous working conditions

▲ economic exploitation of the labor and the culture of people of color

▲ less access to education

▲ more vulnerability to violence

▲ loss of tremendous contributions that people of color can make and have made to the society

▲ fear, mistrust, anger, and violence between whites and people of color

▲ narrowing and distortion of history and current reality among white people

▲ disillusionment, despair, fear, and hopelessness among whites and people of color

▲ denial and suppression of cultural differences among white people

▲ total eradication of certain native cultures

One of the exercises we do with racially mixed groups to understand the effects of racist oppression more clearly is the following.

▲ People of color stand-up

The exercise begins with everyone sitting down. People of color are asked to rise whenever a statement applies to them. A person may pass, but they are asked to notice their feelings if they do. As with other stand-up exercises, facilitators should pay attention to the racial balance and level of safety. This exercise is also effective for people of color support or discussion groups.

The exercise:

Please stand up silently if

1. Your ancestors were forced to come to this country, or were forced to relocate from where they were living in this country —either temporarily or permanently—or were restricted from living in certain areas because of their race or ethnicity

2. You ever heard or overheard people saying that you or your people should leave, go home, or go back where you came from

3. In your family, as a child, you were the intermediary between your parent/s and store clerks or public officials (social workers, school officials, etc.) because of language or other differences

4. You were ever called names or otherwise ridiculed by someone you didn't know because you were African-American, Latino, Asian-American, Native American, Arab-American, or of mixed heritage

5. You were ever ridiculed by a teacher, employer, or supervisor because of your racial heritage

6. You have ever been told by a white person that you are "different" from other people of your racial or ethnic group

7. You were ever told that you didn't act black/Latino/Asian/Arab/Indian ... *enough*

8. You were ever told you were too sensitive about racial matters, or were acting *too* black/Latino/Asian/Arab/Indian ...

9. You have ever been told by a white person that you are too sensitive, too emotional, or too angry when talking about racism

10. You ever received less than full respect, attention, or response from a doctor, police officer, court official, city official, or other professional because of your race or ethnicity

11. You ever saw your racial/ethnic group portrayed on television or in the movies in a derogatory way

12. You ever tried to change your physical appearance (e.g., your hair, skin color), mannerisms, speech, or behavior to avoid being judged or ridiculed because of your race or ethnicity

13. You have ever been told to learn to speak "correct" or "better" English

14. You were ever discouraged or prevented from pursuing academic or work goals, or tracked into a lower vocational level because of your racial or ethnic identity

15. You were ever mistrusted or accused of stealing, cheating, or lying because you were African-American, Latino, Asian-American, Native American, Arab-American, etc.

16. You ever picked up that someone was afraid of you because of your ethnic or racial background

17. You were ever stopped by police on the street because of your racial or ethnic identity

18. You were ever refused employment because of your race or ethnic background

19. You were ever paid less, treated less fairly, or given harder work than a white person in a similar position

20. Your religious or cultural holidays were not recognized on your job or at your school and meetings, and work time were scheduled during those periods

21. You ever were refused housing, were discouraged from applying for housing, or had to leave housing because of racial discrimination

22. You ever felt conspicuous, uncomfortable, or alone in a group because you were the only representative of your racial group

23. You ever felt uncomfortable or angry about a remark or joke made about your race or ethnicity, but didn't feel safe enough to confront it

24. You ever felt the threat of violence because of your race

25. You or close friends or family were ever a victim of violence because of your race

An alternative format is to start out with a couple of these questions and then ask people of color to take turns asking "Please stand up if you ever..." questions of each other, which they create from their own experiences.

To close the exercise, the group processes their feelings about the experience.

Internalized oppression

When people of color are taught, over generations, that they are inferior, they internalize the lies. The patterns of internalized oppression may look different for each racial group: Asian-Americans may sometimes believe they are the "model minority" and should be good in math; Latinos/Latinas may learn that Spanish accents mean lower intelligence; African-Americans may be taught to value light skin, or conversely, worry about whether they are "black enough." The end results are the same, both to pit people of color against themselves and to pit different racial groups against each other.

A word about anti-Semitism

Jewish people are a religious and cultural group. Anti-Semitism is the systematic mistreatment of Jews by Gentiles (non-Jews). Jews are not a racial grouping (there are Latin, Arabic, white, black, and Asian people who are Jewish. In fact, the majority of the people in the world who are Jewish are people of color). However anti-Semitism follows the same structure of oppression and internalized oppression as racism, while having a slightly different slant in the United States.

Although Jews have been historically persecuted in most countries in the world, and have endured the Holocaust in very recent history, the oppression has been made invisible in the United States. Jews are said to not have it so bad here: They have a lot of money, they are very powerful, etc. In other words, the old stereotypes about Jewish people are continued, but the vulnerability to discrimination and violence that Jews experience is denied. In the meantime, Jews experience discrimination daily in Gentile society, whether in direct acts of persecution such as the bombing of synagogues and the desecration of cemeteries, in the jokes, in the invalidation of Jewish culture and Jewish holidays, or in the denial of the oppression itself.

In the United States, Jewish people are, as in other countries, pitted against people of color and blamed for problems the society as a whole has created. They are also told that anti-Semitism doesn't exist. For Jews who are light-skinned (of European descent) there is relative privilege over Jewish and non-Jewish people of color. This in turn separates people of color and European-descended Jews more and sets them up as antagonists.

Alliance: Being a white ally

The devastation that racism produces for people of color, both individually and within their cultures, must be clearly understood by whites. Whites must also understand the social and institutional nature of racism in order to move beyond self-guilt or the blaming of other whites. This understanding also enables us to see that although changing personal views and behaviors is useful, acting to change social practice is where real community building will happen.

Furthermore, for white people who do this work, it is necessary to understand that this is also a white issue—racism is and has been devastating for whites. Whites' early experiences of learning about racism were hurtful, often coming from people they trusted or loved who were passing on their own hurt. Racism also operates to deny the different ethnic heritages of white people, persuading whites they have no cultural heritage, but instead a bland monoculture. Or it assigns different statuses to different white ethnic groups, based upon structures of domination inherited from European culture: Eastern European, Mediterranean, and Irish people are often made "one down" within white society. Racism falsifies their view of the world. It saddles them with resentfulness, unawareness, fear, guilt, or hate when the subject of racism is brought up. And it is necessary to understand that all of these effects are happening to white children now.

The following exercise for white people can help demonstrate just how racist training takes place and what the costs are for whites.

▲ Whites stand-up

White participants are asked to stand up if a statement applies to them, notice who else is standing, and notice their feelings. Everyone has the right to pass, but they are asked to pay attention to how they feel if they do.

The exercise:

Please stand up silently if

1. You don't know exactly what your European/American heritage is, what your great-grandparents' names are, or what regions or cities your ancestors came from

2. You have ever been told or believe you are a "Heinz 57" or a "mutt"

3. a. You grew up in a household where you heard derogatory racial terms or racial jokes
   b. You grew up in a household where you heard that racism was bad, so you were never to notice out loud or comment on racial differences (for example, people told you, "It doesn't matter if you're purple or green, we're all equal, so don't notice a person's color")
   c. You grew up in a household where you heard that racism was bad, that some or all white people were racist, and that you would always have to fight against it

4. You grew up, lived, or live in a neighborhood, or went to school or a camp which, as far as you knew, was exclusively white

5. You grew up with people of color who were servants, maids, gardeners, or babysitters in your house

6. You were ever told not to play with children of a nonwhite ethnicity when you were a child

7. (For this category, after you stand, stay standing if the next item applies to you.) You ever saw pictures or images in magazines, film, or television, or heard in music or on the radio of
   ▲ Mexicans depicted as drunk, lazy, or illiterate
   ▲ Asians depicted as exotic, cruel, or mysterious
   ▲ Asian Indians depicted as excitable or "silly"
   ▲ Arabs depicted as swarthy, ravishing, or "crazed"
   ▲ Black people depicted as violent or criminal
   ▲ Pacific Islanders depicted as funloving or lazy
   ▲ American Indians depicted as drunk, savage, or "noble"
   ▲ character-roles from nonwhite cultures acted by white actors

8. You did not meet people of color in person, or socially, before you were well into your teens

9. You ever find yourself trying to pretend "not to notice" the ethnicity or race or skin color of people of color

10. You ever felt like "white" culture was "wonderbread" culture—empty, boring—or that another racial group had more rhythm, more athletic ability, were better with their hands, better at math and technology, better at trade or handling money, or had more musical or artistic creativity than you

11. You ever felt that people of another racial group were more spiritual than white people

12. You have ever been sexually attracted to a person from another racial group because it seemed exotic, exciting, or a challenge

13. You ever learned to be afraid of or not trust people of a nonwhite racial group

14. You ever felt yourself being nervous or fearful, or stiffening up when encountering people of color in a neutral public situation (e.g., in an elevator or on the street)

15. You ever worked in a place where all the people of color had more menial jobs, were paid less, or were otherwise harassed or discriminated against

16. You ever ate in a public place where all the customers were white, and the people of color who were present were service workers

17. You have ever been in an organization, workgroup, meeting, or event which people of color protested as racist or you knew or suspected to be racist

18. You ever felt racial tension in a situation and were afraid to say anything about it

19. You ever had degrading jokes, comments, or put-downs about people of color made in your presence and felt powerless to protest

20. You ever witnessed people of color being mistreated in any way by white people

21. You ever saw people of color being put down or attacked verbally or physically and did not intervene

22. You ever felt guilty or powerless to do anything about racism

23. You ever felt embarrassed by, separate from, superior to, or more tolerant than other white friends or family members

24. You have ever been in a close friendship or relationship with

another white person where that relationship was damaged or lost because of a disagreement about racism

25. You have ever been in a close friendship or relationship with a person of color where that relationship was affected, endangered by or lost because of racism between you or from others

26. You are not in a close significant relationship with any people of color in your life right now

This exercise ends with the group breaking into dyads to discuss how they felt during the exercise. A whole group discussion can then follow.

After the exercise, someone may ask "Are you saying that all white people are racist?" Let's be clear: no one is born a racist, and no one is born inferior. It takes years to train children to believe the lies and to pass on violence to people of other colors. It takes years to train people of color that they are less able than white people. Young white people resist these lies as best as they can. But with an entire culture training them, many end up believing and passing on the lies. Young people of color also resist the lies and violence as best they can. But the oppression takes its toll, and many end up internalizing it.

For adults working with young people on racism

The situation is not hopeless. Every day we fight back and see others fighting back against the realities of racism. To strengthen ourselves in this struggle, there are some things we can do.

It is crucial for adults who work with children who are white, Jewish, and of color, often in the same classroom or group, to be completely clear about what racism is, what anti-Semitism is, and how they operate to divide us from one another. In fact, it is doubly important, because adult society elsewhere is actively feeding these children lies and confusions about racism. This means several things for adult workers:

1. We must be able to identify how racism operates and affects *us* from day to day, looking at our own ethnic heritages, our early memories of learning about other groups, and areas where we might get stuck when issues are flying in the classroom.

2. We must be prepared to initiate frank and open dialogue about racism in the classroom. This contradicts young people's experience in a society where adults often pretend racism doesn't exist

or have great ambivalence about discussing it. We have also noticed over the years that racism will not be addressed in class unless adults bring it up; teens' experience of adults' volatility and denial makes them reluctant to risk discussion. But once the issue comes up, the discussion takes off.

3. We must ensure that cultural diversity is represented in our numbers—that whites and people of color are all working together and modeling cooperative relationships for young people. Because we are working within white-dominated institutions this is not easy, of course. But racism damages all of us, and will continue to damage all liberation work with young people until we address it head-on.

4. In order to work effectively with young people on sexism, we need to understand the effect of racial oppression in their lives and enable them to heal from its violence as well. Each oppression is a system; the oppressions altogether are an interlocking system. One will not be lessened while others, with their own sets of abuses and hopelessnesses, are left in place. This means making racial issues a part of all classroom work, naming them, interweaving them in roleplays and exercises, and never "forgetting" to address them.

5. We can acknowledge the strong and powerful things we and others are doing to end racism.

6. We need not blame ourselves for racism, or for times when we failed to do more. Blame isn't useful for us, and it's absolutely useless for young people. Nothing is quite as useless to women as guilty men, as useless to people of color as guilty whites, or as useless to children as guilty adults.

7. We can make mistakes, fix them, take responsibility for our actions, analyze and learn from them, and go forward.

8. We can assume that no one wants to participate in this racist system. Everyone is doing the best they can with the lies and ignorance they were given.

9. We can recognize that we all come from cultural and ethnic traditions. By taking pride in our own, we are less likely to fear and attack others (see page 23, "For the power group").

10. We can examine how we learned about racial difference and discrimination through early experiences and impressions, and give healing attention to what was hurtful.

There are potentially endless exercises and techniques for doing personal work on combating racism. This manual contains several, like the Power Shuffle and Power Chart (pages 14, 16). Since we experience and learn the system in groups, from and with those around us, it is particularly powerful to *unlearn* it with others. Working in multiracial groups to end racism is perhaps the most effective way of all to counteract our training.

Safety

Like sexism, issues of racism have great emotional pain attached to them. Creating emotional safety among people we work with has to be of prime importance in designing our work.

There must be safety for people of color so that

▲ they do not become targets of further abuse

▲ they do not become isolated from the group

▲ they are not set up to be spokespeople for their race or ethnic identity

▲ they can do their personal work of healing and becoming more powerful

There must also be safety for white people so that

▲ they can get in touch with and heal from the lies of the early painful "learning" process they have had

▲ they are not faulted for what they have been told and can honestly bring up doubts, confusion, anger, and other painful emotions

▲ they can listen attentively and supportively to people of color speaking out

▲ they can support and challenge each other to continue working on this issue

Finally, safety comes for all groups when adults are clear and the information presented is direct, basic, and consistent. If we can create safety for the process, each young person will become clearer, stronger, and closer to others. The group itself will take on safety, interest, and strength to end racism within the group and within the larger society.

The work to end racism goes hand in hand with the work to end male/female violence—just as it joins efforts to stop anti-Semitism, violence against gays, lesbians, and bisexuals, the elderly, working-class, and poor, to name some other targets of oppression. It is part of our lifework to help young people create a world that is safe, empowering, and based upon liberation, equality, and respect for all of us.

OUT PROUD: UNLEARNING HETEROSEXISM

by Allan Creighton

Probably the most routinely explosive subject that comes up in the group or classroom is gay/lesbian identity. Typically it comes up when we talk about the "Act-Like-A-Man" Box and the "Act-Like-A-Lady" Flower and the names boys and girls are called when they attempt to act outside them (see Section 4). When students call out some of the names—"gay," "fag," "dyke," or "queer"—the discomfort is palpable: giggling, side conversations, finger-pointing. Other things happen too:

▲ immediate disclaiming of lesbian or gay identity, sometimes verbal ("Well, I'm not gay, but . . ."), sometimes physical (shifts in posture or voice levels to appear more "manly" or "womanly")

▲ questioning the facilitators about their sexual identities

▲ adopting a detached attitude, as if lesbians and gays were an odd species and required sanction from others even to exist ("I don't care what they do behind closed doors, but . . .")

▲ presuming that everyone (at least every youth) in the room is heterosexual or has no questions about her/his own sexual identity

▲ and, not infrequently, expressing violent disgust

As facilitators, we can easily get hooked into the same anxiety. We may subtly or openly identify at once as heterosexual (regardless of our sexual orientations) with the same sort of cues, or rush to bury, drop, or change the subject. Somehow the discussion, once the subject of "gay" comes up, never quite returns to where it was. What is this anxiety about?

A classic word for it is "homophobia," a dislike, disdain, or even hatred of homosexuals rooted in fear, really a panic, about closeness among members of the same sex. This panic is learned, not biological or instinctive. It is also the source of the astounding level of violence

surrounding this issue among youth. That violence we call heterosexism.

Some definitions

Heterosexuality is sexual attraction to or sexual activity with the
other sex; homosexuality is sexual attraction to or sexual activity with
the same sex; bisexuality is sexual attraction to or sexual activity with
both sexes. It is now standard to use the term "gay" for men who are
homosexual and "lesbian" for women who are homosexual as a
further distinction.

Here are some facts to consider:

1. There is no generalization that can be made about how (or
    whether) one is or becomes lesbian or gay or bisexual—or
    heterosexual. Each occurs normally, with no identifiable cause,
    and occurs differently for different people.

2. All cultural groups (people of different ethnicities, ages, and so
    forth) at all times in history have had gay and lesbian, as well
    as heterosexual, members.

3. At a minimum, one in ten people are gay or lesbian, and more
    are bisexual. Human sexuality studies conducted by Kinsey
    (which are dated and may underrepresent the facts) reported
    that overall at least 37% of us have had same-sex sexual en-
    counters—up to 50% of adult men, 28% of women, 60% of boys,
    and 33% of girls.

4. There are as many ways of being gay or lesbian as there are of
    being heterosexual, just as there are many ways of being male or
    female. This means that gay men as a group are no more
    "feminine" than other men, and lesbians are no more "mas-
    culine" than other women. Masculinity and femininity are not
    measures of sexual orientation.

5. Not all people are either straight *or* gay. Many of us are bisexual,
    and many of us are elsewhere on the continuum of sexual
    orientation. Some of us change orientation over the course of our
    lives; others don't. That is to say, human sexuality *is* a con-
    tinuum of orientations and attractions. Exclusive heterosexuality
    and homosexuality are two convenient social definitions but fall
    far short of describing the range of human sexual interaction.

The oppression

Heterosexism is the systematic, day-to-day, institutional mistreatment of gay, lesbian, and bisexual people by a heterosexually dominated culture. We are expanding its meaning from the usual one, a belief that heterosexual practices and lifestyles are superior, to include the types of oppression that are associated with other "isms." Homophobia is one of heterosexism's major expressions, a way each of us—whether heterosexual or lesbian, gay or bisexual—carries the oppression in ourselves.

Heterosexism is one of the few oppressions that is legal; i.e., to be homosexual is illegal in many places. Twenty-eight states criminalize same-sex partnerships with anti-sodomy laws. In virtually all jurisdictions in the United States, same-sex domestic partners cannot be legally married or expect to secure custody rights or visitation with children from divorced partners, or obtain tax breaks. Gays, lesbians, and bisexuals can be prohibited, or dishonorably discharged, from military service and the Boy Scouts. They can also be discriminated against in housing and in employment. For example, lesbian/gay identity could cost a public school teacher, hospital worker, or childcare worker her or his job. This amounts to nothing less than a denial of basic civil rights and unequal protection under the law.

Every American institution, from the family to the church to therapy to the high school prom to Top-40 radio, contains the presumption that we are all heterosexual. This presumption of "normal" sexuality is nowhere enforced so powerfully as in the family itself. If you face oppression in the larger society as a person of color, a disabled person, or a worker, you may be able to find people in your family who will support you; but it is exactly in coming out to your family that you can expect to experience immediate and severe abuse.

The presumption of heterosexuality makes gayness invisible and conceals homosexuality behind anxiety-ridden stereotypes. Some of these stereotypes are that gays proselytize, that same-sex child molesters are gay, that AIDS is a gay disease, or that gayness comes from excessive mothering or is a simple matter of choice (or the opposite: that all sexual orientation is innate, having to do with brain chemistry), or that lesbians just haven't met the right man.

Beyond invisibility is stigma, found both in the medical treatment of homosexuality as an aberrant mental condition and in the religious demonizing of gayness as a moral evil to be exorcised. Stigma is motivated by larger moral anxieties and myths about sexuality that dominate American life. Sex is still a morally frowned-upon activity and a forbidden topic in most classrooms and living rooms, so it becomes an obsession for all of us. The alternatives youth are given to cope with the obsession—to repress sexual feelings or to act them out—are set along exclusively heterosexual lines. Even the idea of questioning one's sexual identity out loud is prohibited to teens because it is too dangerous to consider.

And finally, violence. The label of "queer" or "dyke" is one of the most physically dangerous to carry in a high school setting. A boy can start a fight to the death just by calling another boy "fag." And as gays become more outspoken and visible, the rate and intensity of gay-bashings climbs. Overall, gays and lesbians are seven times more likely to be assaulted than heterosexuals. The historical precedents extend from European witch burnings to extermination of lesbians and gays in the Nazi Holocaust.

Ultimately this violence touches all of us; each of us can be targeted by heterosexism. It is rooted in the socialization that every child receives. Gay or lesbian is exactly what you cannot be if you are supposed to "act like a man" or are a "total woman," as defined by the dominant culture. In fact, it is crucial to the formation of this "real man" identity that rage against homosexuals be forged in young boys and teenagers. So, at any time—on the street, in the classroom, at my work or in my family—I can be called gay or lesbian and attacked, whatever my sexual orientation. If I speak out against sexism, or racism, or any injustice, my voice can at once be neutralized if I am labeled a queer. Think of the physical behaviors alone that each of us has learned to perform when in public, on a daily basis, to avoid being labeled as gay or lesbian. Think about how we negotiate physical contact with members of the same sex, how we carry ourselves, how we dress, how we walk, how we sit in a chair, what we joke about. Then think about how some of these have become so automatic that we don't even think of them.

Internalized oppression

Some of the effects of heterosexism and homophobia are internalized by lesbian, gay, and bisexual people. The ways in which homosexuality has been penalized as a crime, medicalized as a disease, or preached against as a sin have made self-doubt, guilt, shame, outright denial of one's identity, or attacks upon other gays a common feature of lesbian/gay life. One must decide a dozen times a day whether to come out or not—in class, at the office, at the market, on the bus, in the congregation, at home. The absolute intolerance of homosexuality in most youth settings makes for the ultimate internalization: adolescent lesbians and gays account for one-third of teens committing suicide. None of these actions, of course, is part of being lesbian, gay, or bisexual; all are caused by attempts to survive in a hostile environment.

Vibrant lesbian and gay cultures have always existed, challenging dominant paradigms of social behavior, taking leading roles in battles for civil rights and women's liberation, thriving in political, social, creative, and religious communities, sustaining alternative families and healthy parenting, and, most recently, emerging as the gay liberation and feminist movements. All of this must be recognized, remembered, celebrated, and called upon when we think about internalized oppression.

Alliance: Working with young people on heterosexism

As adults committed to young people's liberation we must decide, regardless of personal or religious beliefs or feelings, and regardless of our own sexual orientations, that discrimination and violence against gays, lesbians, and bisexuals must be stopped. Making this decision means stating publicly that this violence is wrong. Challenging heterosexism creates safety not only for young people of these identities and others who are questioning their sexuality, but also for heterosexual youth being pressured to be violent to "prove" their identities.

We can broadly agree that discrimination by race, gender, physical ability, and the like should be eliminated. But since most of us possess insufficient information about what heterosexism is, it is incumbent upon each of us to examine our own convictions and the assumptions that prevent us from accepting differing sexual identities.

A good place to begin is with any early experiences we remember of learning that closeness between

Unity Photo: Ben Ferris ©1992

men or between women has strict boundaries. We could look particularly at early religious teachings we may have received. How did these experiences affect us or limit our activity? Whatever our sexual orientation is, how do these experiences affect our work with youth now?

The next step is to strategize how to address these issues in our work with youth. Based on our experience, it is best to develop classes, workshops, and groups devoted explicitly to unlearning heterosexism, facilitated by lesbian/gay and heterosexual presenters. This can be done in tandem with the programs on sexism, racism, and adultism outlined in this book. In workshops on heterosexism for both young adults and adults, we often use the exercises below.

▲ Coming out roleplay

One facilitator plays an older teen or young adult who is lesbian or gay, unknown to her/his parents. Two others (or one other plus a teen volunteer) play the parents. The father and youth are in the driveway, working on a car (or in the living room, watching television). The father pressures the young person about who she/he is dating, and the latter finally decides to come out. The father reacts explosively. The mother enters, finds out what is going on, and chimes in with her shock and disapproval.

This is an *interactive* roleplay. After the first few minutes, participants are encouraged to come up, tap any one of the characters on the shoulder, and take his or her place. Make sure that each of the parts gets replacement actors and that the lesbian/gay character doesn't devolve into a stereotype. After a few minutes, the roleplay is stopped and the group processes how it felt.

Alternative scenarios you may want to try include a worker coming out to two unsupportive friends on the job, or a teen coming out to two disapproving friends from school. The point is for participants to try out the roles and for lots of feelings to be aired. Facilitators should ensure that (as in reality for many gay/lesbian youth) at least one "parent" at some point threatens extreme violence and orders the youth out of the house.

This can lead to a general discussion about what heterosexism is, its connections with sexism, and the conditioning young people receive to be heterosexual.

If we determine that the group has a fair amount of safety, for example if they are close friends or coworkers, have made a commitment to work on this issue, or have accepted "out" lesbians or gays among them, we may next try the following exercise.

▲ Closeness dyad

Participants are separated into same-sex dyads (pairs). Dyads arrange themselves so that partners can hold hands, or sit in one another's laps, or lie back in one another's arms. They take timed turns, three minutes each way, talking about how it feels to do this.

At the end of this exercise, the whole group discusses what came up, including feelings of discomfort and early messages about homophobia. Permit lots of processing time for these exercises, and close with some commitments from the group about unlearning heterosexism.

Some practical guidelines

In doing this work, we have developed certain approaches in our teen classes and groups addressing gender and racial violence. These are given below.

1. Assume, act, and speak as if there are lesbian, gay, bisexual, or questioning youth present. Notice any tendency to presume that everyone is heterosexual.

2. Continue to raise the issue of heterosexism wherever you mention the other "isms." Much of heterosexism is about silencing and hiding. So it is always appropriate to discuss it and to be prepared for feelings that come up—not only young people's and other adults' but your own.

3. Always question or interrupt derogatory or joking uses of the words "queer," "fag," "dyke." It is important to remember that young people who use these words are not simply being abusive, nor are they simply being funny. The names and accompanying behavior are about fear that has been instilled in them. Leaving this unchallenged lowers everyone's safety.

4. Assume that if you are heterosexual you also lack information on this issue. Research lesbian, gay, and bisexual history and consult the abundant new writings by lesbian, gay, and bisexual people in various cultures and races about their experience. Provide as much of this information to young people as possible and don't fault them for not having it previously.

5. If you are heterosexual, in a situation where you are spontaneously asked what your sexual identity is avoid as much as possible identifying your own sexual orientation. Identifying as heterosexual may silence and separate gay/lesbian or ques-

tioning youth who are present. It is fine to return the question, asking them why they want to know, how it feels not to know, etc. Use this as a chance for young people to express and question their fear or concern and to talk about the dangers of "coming out." (Practice this response, *a lot*, ahead of time.)

6. If you are lesbian, gay, or bisexual, you may decide, on strategically picked occasions, that it is appropriate to be out. There is a power in being out to young people from the beginning. Most young people have never been allowed to meet an "out" adult, and it can be a crucial experience in pride, understanding, and self-assertion for them. However this is a choice, based on your gauge of your safety.

7. Evaluate your program not only for anti-gay/lesbian/bisexual violence, but for the missing connections between heterosexism and sexism. We cannot effectively address male violence unless we speak to the homophobia that keeps it in place.

In the last analysis, no oppression is lessened if any is left in place. Try what you can, make mistakes, and try again. Every attempt will make more room where lesbian, bisexual, and gay youth and adults can be out proud.

THOUGHTS ON CLASS
by Paul Kivel

Many of us are drawn to this work because it allows us to care and advocate for those who have less power and opportunity than we do—young people. Some of us have become social workers, teachers, probation officers, child protection workers, medical professionals, therapists, counselors, and other providers of educational services to youth. Most of us have a little more education and a little more job privilege, if not money, than many of the young people and their families with whom we interact. Most important, we have the ability to make decisions and interpret the institutional rules that affect the lives of those we "serve." In these roles, if not in background, we are a "middle" class, operating between society's institutions and the people under the institutions.

From this perspective, let's look at the ways in which our work functions within the systems of class and economic relationships in this country. We don't make decisions about where jobs are located and who will get them. We don't decide what kind of healthcare system and other benefits are available. We are not responsible for how much money gets spent on education and what educational programs get priority. The ruling class of this country—the people and institutions which shape our communities and much of our daily lives—determine the context of our work. Within that context, what purpose does our work serve? Whom does it really benefit?

In order to keep our economy producing profits that can continue to be accumulated by the wealthy, our economic system is set up to keep some people on call for periodic low-wage labor, others for regular low-wage labor, while still others are left out of the labor market completely. For this set-up to work smoothly, there has to be a way to contain the potentially restless and explosive power of people whose labor earns them little and who survive in poverty.

The containment part of our economy has four components, and all of us in the middle class are instrumental in maintaining them. The first component is hope—the belief that the system is flexible and that anyone can make it up the ladder of success. The second is self-blame, which leads people to believe that if they don't succeed it is because of their individual failure. The third component is a welfare system that provides poorer people with just enough so they can stay alive, physically functional, and sane enough not to disrupt the rest of society. The backup component to these three is physical and legal enforcement of the roles and relationships when the first three components break down.

For people to think they or their children have a chance to escape poverty, unemployment, low wages, high rent, and the violent conditions in their lives, they need to see a few people make it from their situation to a better one. Regardless of the reality, they need to believe that if they have it together, work hard, and persevere they can succeed. Success, in this way, often becomes synonymous with escaping from family, class, ethnic, racial, and neighborhood backgrounds. One of our tasks as workers and educators is to choose the best and the brightest from disempowered groups and push them up the ladder. We are supposed to encourage them to stay in school, study hard, and become leaders. Education is the key.

The reality is that those who do make it out of poverty leave their communities and join the middle class, leaving *their* communities unchanged. These few success stories foster the illusion of hope and keep our work focused on helping people escape, one by one. They also distract us from understanding why there is unequal economic opportunity in the first place.

These stories of individual achievement serve another purpose—they provide a way to blame those who don't make it. It appears that success goes to the hard-working, disciplined, competitive, smart, correct-English-speaking, and self-confident. Those who don't succeed believe it is their own fault: if only they worked a little harder, were smarter, etc. Self-blame is reinforced by the many professionals ready to step in with training in self-esteem, assertiveness, self-management, and other achievement skills. The fact that the economic system is set up to allow only a few people through the gates to success is kept carefully hidden.

We live in a society in which women are told they are not as smart as men. Most people of color are told they cannot compete with whites in the classroom; Asian-Americans are told not to compete so much. Working-class youth are told to go only for job-training skills and basic education. Increased self-esteem and other personal skills are only going to help a few people stand up to the constant harassment, stereotyping, low expectations, and limited opportunities available to them.

The hope fades for some before or during early adolescence. For others, it happens later in adult life. It makes no difference whether they blame themselves, their family, community, or cultural group. Angry and hurt, they just try to survive.

Yet surviving economically takes so much time, energy, and emotional resource that people are often unable to take any action to change the circumstances that produce the lack of opportunity in the first place. Those of us in the middle class who dole out the food stamps, welfare, and social security "benefits," green cards, and healthcare often do so in such a way that recipients are left drained from the bureaucratic gymnastics and all the monitoring they are subjected to. Very little organized resistance to the economic system is possible under these circumstances. Just think of the powerlessness in the names: "client," "patient," "dependent," "recipient."

The social service sector, as broadly as I have defined it, encourages hope, reinforces failure, and minimally sustains life. These three functions, properly fulfilled, keep the system of power and money very stable. In case of malfunction, some of us are trained to enforce the system by punishing and monitoring the "troublemakers." Deans and principals, probation officers, police, welfare investigators, and psychiatrists—each are empowered to intervene punitively in the lives of people who are disruptive.

It is not accidental that women hold jobs in the first three categories and men hold jobs in the enforcement area. Women are trained to take care of people, to nurture and support, to be helpers. Men are trained to be tough and aggressive and to use violence to control others. There is nothing biological in these functions; it is a division of labor by social role. Both roles are very useful in maintaining a system where a small group of people control most of the wealth of our country, leaving the rest of us with very little. (According to U.S. Government figures, ½% of the population owns 29.4% of the wealth in this country, while 90% of the population owns 24.3%.)

Each of us who does not want to play out our preassigned role has to explore how we can work to change an economic structure that consigns so many of us to poverty and impoverished lives. We must constantly remind ourselves that we are all in this together. Any temporary middle-class privilege, power, or status we have is very fragile. A major medical crisis, a disability, or cash flow problem quickly reminds us of our economic vulnerability.

It is also important to acknowledge that we have socially sanctioned power over people's lives. Some of us through our work can take children from families, provide or deny benefits, allow or prohibit access to various programs and community resources, and recommend people for jobs, housing, or academic placement. Let's be up-front with ourselves and each other about this fact. Let's use the power we have in the best interests of those whose lives we affect, as *they* define *their* interests.

We can help people have better lives, but unless we are part of a social movement for change, we are not moving toward a more equitable and economically democratic society. One way to do this is to question all the assumptions we have about young people so that we don't put them down for their situations or blame them for the results of the economic, racial, and gender-based distribution of resources and opportunities. Another way is to help confront people's internalized self-blame, self-destructiveness, and violence by providing support and alternatives rather than excusing such actions, and by helping them understand the costs (emotional, physical, and economic) of these counterproductive patterns.

Incorporating education about the system of political power into our work helps to break the cycle of self-blame. It also helps tremendously when we can organize with groups of people to work together to take the power. For example, we can enable students to see themselves as allies rather than competitors and enemies. We can aid welfare recipients in organizing themselves for greater strength and mutual support. Finally, it is important that we examine our own needs for power and security to ensure that they're not acted out against the people we want to help. For example, if we are taught in daily headlines that our own income and work is in continual jeopardy, and then told that "welfare cheats" are the problem, there are many ways we can abuse and blame the people with whom we work. We must not let our own feelings of anger, frustration, or powerlessness lead us to hurt others.

We are also vulnerable and dependent because we too need jobs, references, and benefits. The system uses the same three tools of hope, self-blame, and controlled distribution of benefits to keep *us* playing *our* roles. If we get out of line, there's plenty of punitive apparatus in place. We can be reprimanded, disciplined, put on probation, or just plain fired, which returns us to the frightening role of "client." We each must heed someone with authority over us who may encourage us to pass on abuse to those with less power.

We can only stop this cycle of economic violence if we build alliances with co-workers and those we serve in the community. First, we have to see that what is happening to others is also happening to us. We can become allies for others by responding to their needs. We can tell them what resources and services we can provide and then let them decide what they want us to do for them. We must constantly ask ourselves whose side we are on: are we working to maintain the system for the wealthy or to change the system for poor and working-class adults and youth? The latter leads us to organize not just for higher wages and better healthcare but also for the power to change the way people are able to meet their needs.

Many of us were drawn to our work because we wanted to do something in our communities. If we keep a wide perspective, balancing our personal needs with working together to build a different kind of society, there is much we can do.

ADULTISM
by Paul Kivel

Why do young people do poorly in school? Why do young people use drugs, or hang out on street corners, or get pregnant? A common answer to these questions is that many teens have low self-esteem, generally defined as a poor sense of one's worth or ability—a lack of confidence. Professional literature about adolescents, social service priorities, and funding trends all emphasize programs which build self-esteem.

Is the problem low self-esteem?

When I think back to my years as a teenager, I notice how much I wanted to do and how little power I had to do it. I wanted to go places I couldn't; I wanted to try to do things I wasn't supposed to.

I wanted to affect and change my classes, my community, my neighborhood, and I wasn't able to. I never had the money, wheels, friends, influence, or credibility to make a difference.

There were lots of promises from adults. If you study hard, work hard, stay out of fights, stay safe, don't have sex, don't drink or smoke, don't mess up, adults promised you a life filled with power and privileges. But the promise of power 10 or 20 years in the future was not inviting or convincing. In the meantime, few adults listened to me, allowed me to participate, trusted me, or noticed me and my friends and fellow students.

Of course, when adults systematically don't notice you, listen to you, trust you, or allow you to participate in making meaningful decisions, your sense of self-worth deteriorates. When they grade you continually on your academic performance, your concept of your value can hinge on it too. If, on top of this, they belittle you, punish you arbitrarily, yell at you, put you down, beat you, or molest you, your self-esteem can plummet.

Oppression: the issue is power

Our problem as young people was not low self-esteem. Rather, we had no power over our lives. Without power to protect ourselves, we were constantly restricted, disrespected, and abused by adults. At home, at school, in stores, at work, on the sports field, on the streets—adults had the authority to decide how we should dress, how we should talk, where we could be, and who we could be with. They decided our future, through discipline, records, arrests, report cards, evaluations, allowances, and/or the lack or neglect of all of the above.

Teens face the same lack of power today. Adults make promises to them. Adolescence should be a time of promise, of open futures, of the possibility of meaningful education, fully remunerated work, and healthy relationships. The reality is a broken promise: limited education, unemployment and underemployment, unplanned families, dysfunctional relationships, and an epidemic of violence.

Internalized oppression

And teens are still blamed for failure. Adults label them troublemakers, irresponsible, immature, apathetic, lazy, dishonest, underachievers, and stupid. Adults define this failure as a personal problem for each teen, a failure of self-esteem, and teens end up blaming themselves or attacking each other. Teen violence—the teen-to-teen abuse that happens in gangs, in couples, or from the school bully; the self-abuse from drugs or alcohol; unwanted pregnancy; suicide—all of these can be seen as forms of learned helplessness and hopelessness in teens. These are ways in which, because of abuse from adults, they have learned to give up on themselves.

To check on the experience of adultism among teenagers, we sometimes use the following visualization in the classroom.

▲ Adultism visualization
by Allan Creighton

Group participants, regardless of age, think of themselves as young people, close their eyes, and pay attention to their feelings as the facilitator, playing an "adult," throws out the following statements in an increasingly angry and abusive tone:

- ▲ Not now. I don't have time.
- ▲ You're too young to understand.
- ▲ We'll talk about it later.
- ▲ Go to your room.
- ▲ Not until you finish your homework.
- ▲ Clean your plate.
- ▲ I work my fingers to the bone for you.
- ▲ Wait till you have children.
- ▲ Wait till your father gets home.
- ▲ When I was your age, I had it a *lot* harder.
- ▲ Do what I say.
- ▲ Not in my house you don't.
- ▲ Because I said so.
- ▲ Sit up. Sit up straight.
- ▲ Don't you talk back to me.
- ▲ Is that the best you can do?
- ▲ You're just a kid.
- ▲ Pay attention when I'm talking to you.

- ▲ You're stupid.

- ▲ Shut up.

- ▲ You show me some respect.

- ▲ This hurts me more than it hurts you.

- ▲ Don't tell your mother about this; it's just our secret.

- ▲ You get right upstairs and change into something decent.

- ▲ Turn off the goddamned TV.

- ▲ Get the hell out of here.

- ▲ All right, *now* you're gonna get what's coming to you.

- ▲ I brought you into this world—I can take you out.

At the close of this exercise, the facilitator has participants open their eyes and take part in the following exercise.

▲ Teen stand-up
by Allan Creighton

The facilitator reads the following statements to the group. For each statement, participants are to stand silently if the statement applies to them as young people, notice who else standing, and notice their feelings, whether standing or sitting. Again, make sure there are enough young people in an age-mixed group for them to be safe.

The exercise:

Please stand up silently if

1. You have ever been called a name by an older person

2. Your dress or appearance was ever criticized by an adult

3. You have ever been called "stupid" or been made to feel less intelligent by an adult

4. An adult ever ignored you, served you last, or watched you suspiciously in a store

5. You have ever been told you were too young to understand

6. Your personal privacy was invaded in any way by an adult

7. You have ever been lied to by an adult

8. You have ever been cheated out of money by an adult

9. You were ever paid less than an adult for doing equal work

10. You were ever stopped by the police on the street

11. You were ever arrested or made part of the juvenile justice system

12. You have ever seen an adult you know personally acting under the influence of drugs or alcohol

13. An adult refused to hold, hug, or show you affection when you wanted them to

14. You were left for a long period of time, or left alone when you didn't want to be, or abandoned by an adult

15. You have ever been physically restrained, trapped, or put on restriction by an adult

16. You were ever yelled at by an adult

17. An adult has ever physically threatened you

18. You have ever been held or touched by an adult in a sexual way when you didn't want to be

19. You have ever been hit or beaten by an adult

At the close of the exercise, the facilitator groups participants into pairs to discuss what came up for them. Then he/she conducts a group discussion on the same question.

We have failed them

This exercise predictably brings up many experiences and many feelings for young people. When we use it with adult groups, the same intense responses occur. Clearly adultism is part of the daily experience of all young people. In reality, we have failed them. We discriminate against teens, keep them unemployed, vulnerable to abuse, exposed to violence and drugs, and uninformed about health and reproductive issues. Then we blame them if they get strung out on drugs. We blame them if they get pregnant or get someone else pregnant. We blame them if they drop out of school or get picked up for hanging out.

And beyond teens' powerlessness in an adult-defined world, actual abuse keeps them from succeeding. Current national estimates are that one out of four girls and one out of six boys is sexually abused. The rates of physical, sexual, and emotional abuse and neglect toward young people are alarming. The Centers for Disease

Control report that violence against children—which can range from throwing an object to using a weapon—occurs in 62% of American families every year. Past experiences of personal violence drastically limit a young person's ability to succeed in the future by fostering self-doubt, mistrust, withdrawal, and self-destructive behavior.

Teens also correctly perceive that if they are a person of color, a woman, gay or lesbian, have a disability, or come from a poorer family, their opportunities to achieve are severely limited. For example, girls face lower expectations and sexual harassment. Black and Latino males face higher rates of institutional discipline, suspensions, and arrests. Gay and lesbian teens have to deal with physical and verbal attacks and intimidation. Teenagers learn to blame themselves for this abuse as well.

When we only help them develop higher self-esteem, we lie to teens. We lead them to believe that they are the problem and they are to blame. We mislead them into thinking that personal virtue, effort, perseverance, and skill can completely change their lives. The reality is that many will fail. Their chances of surviving and succeeding are increased when they know what they are up against. Then they can work together, with us as allies, to change the odds.

▲ How Adults Can Stop Adultism

▲ Be an ally.
Teens need to see us as strong, reliable, and completely on their side, knowing that we trust them, respect them, and will tell them the truth.

▲ Tell the truth about power.
Teens need us to tell them about how power is used and abused in this society—to be informed, clear, and firm about how racism, sexism, adultism, and the other "isms" work. We must be ready to share that information openly and in clear, direct language that does not fault them for lacking information.

▲ Tell the truth about violence.
We also must help them identify the social violence directed at them because they are women, people of color, gay and lesbian, poor, and young. Confirming this reality for them can help them to begin to take power to stop the violence.

▲ Support healing.
We need to let them know that it is not their fault that they have

been demeaned, assaulted, or discriminated against, and that it happens to many of us. We need to pass on skills to them for avoiding further violence in their lives.

▲ Interrupt adultism.
It is always appropriate to intervene supportively where young people's rights or due respect are being denied by adults.

▲ Interrupt internalized adultism.
It is always appropriate to intervene—supportively—when one teen puts down or devalues another, or her/himself.

▲ Promote true history.
Young people need information about their struggles and achievements as young people, so they can take pride in and build upon them. This directs them to think of themselves as a community responsible for one another's well-being.

▲ Be a partner.
Teens need us to be willing to share the power and work with them.

▲ Make mistakes openly and without self-deprecation.
Adults, of course, are never supposed to make mistakes. This can mean we never take the chance to reach that young person who is hardest to get to. Go ahead. Try anyway. And when you make a mistake, it's OK. Just fix it, and try again.

▲ Don't do it alone.
Take other adults with you, and train them to support you when your own issues come up, when you feel you've made a mistake, and so forth. The flip side of the mistreatment of teens is the isolation of adults. Getting support from other adults will help decrease the possibility of taking out your hurt on young people or trying to enlist support from them when they shouldn't have to be in a position to give it.

▲ Trust them to be powerful.
This is about to be their world. They are strong, and have convictions and experience about what is right and what is wrong. Support and expect them to make their own decisions. Nothing will change until they do.

▲ Celebrate their successes.
Every day each teen makes dozens of choices to value their own thinking, relationships, preferences, desires, etc. Every teen finds ways to communicate that the oppression is hurting them, and

every teen finds ways to express love even to those adults passing on the oppression. Every teen finds ways to get attention. These are all victories. Young people also often have to choose between limited options, and their choices are the exercise of will to minimize the oppression. They deserve adult allies who notice and point out these acts of self-determination and celebrate them.

We can be strong and powerful adult allies to young people if we can shift our emphasis from raising their self-esteem to *increasing their power*. That, in turn, will allow the exuberance, insight, and creativity of young people to contribute to bettering all our lives.

Section 3

Being in the Classroom

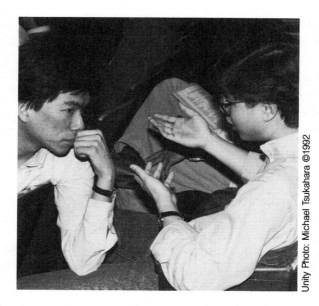

Unity Photo: Michael Tsukahara ©1992

Beyond what we teach is how we teach it. This section speaks to the "how." "Teaching as an Activity" discusses overall strategies for managing a classroom process. "Workshop Goals" is a checklist of assumptions we have found helpful in thinking about how education of young people should work. Finally, "Myths and Facts" discusses a particular, traditional workshop exercise that has often been used in teaching young people about sexual violence, pointing out how the exercise fails and what we must do differently.

TEACHING AS AN ACTIVITY
by Allan Creighton

Walking into a classroom, workshop presenters are entering an institution. An architectural institution, of course—a room, with desks, chairs, a board, artificial light, a front and a back of the room, a teacher's place, in a building of many similar rooms. But also a legal institution, a place where youth are supposed to be during certain hours of the day, certain days of the week, certain months of the year. A social institution, one of the few locales in which teens are permitted to be with each other as a group, and to have relationships with adults not based upon family or local community connections. And a political institution, where adults are charged with the keeping, supervising, and training of youth to become productive and law-abiding adults in the larger society.

How do young people learn here? And what do they learn?

The banking concept of education

The Brazilian educator Paulo Freire has described one traditional model of education: the student, or more graphically the student's head or brain, is a deposit-box, a "bank," into which the teacher makes deposits of discrete bits of knowledge—the periodic table, the battle of Waterloo, how to enter a DOS command, the life-cycle of the paramecium. The teacher must be an expert in a field, a lone expositor of accumulated information. The communication—the deposit—moves in one direction. What is communicated is "outside" the student, in a separate world, impersonal, made up of hard and fast "facts."

Education is an investment, a passing on of the wealth. To learn is to accumulate as much wealth as you can and to be able at any time to display it. After so many deposits, so much wealth, you can get a monthly balance statement: the report card. The seats have built-in desktops, placing and bounding the student, while making a surface to write down, line by line, the facts to ingest and emit on a test.

The classroom might look like this:

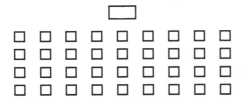

Obviously many classrooms are arranged differently; obviously many other kinds of teaching occur. But our educational system, our method of performance evaluation (grading), and the arrangement of school grades and "tracking" of students into college-bound and noncollege-bound segments turn people into containers to be filled, the world into bite-size objects to fill them with, and education into the process of making deposits.

The hidden curriculum

What do young people actually learn, beyond the unrelated data or "deposits?" Education reformers have for years used the term "hidden curriculum" to describe what youth learn just by virtue of being present in a school, sitting in the room schematized above. Among the teachings of the hidden curriculum—and any of us can add our own recollections of what we learned—are:

▲ obey

▲ be on time

▲ work on a schedule

▲ dress appropriately

▲ behave appropriately

▲ compete

▲ make money

▲ have a career, and if not, expect to be a failure

▲ take tests

▲ follow leaders

▲ belong

▲ learning is memorizing

▲ knowledge is a set of data that can be learned and repeated

▲ I am accountable for my behavior

▲ the mark of success is the achievement of a lifestyle

▲ there is a normal lifestyle that is most desirable, and it can be measured in part by what I own and what services I can command

▲ there are problems in society, and these problems have to do with individual acts, with individuals doing the wrong thing

▲ I am capable of having or causing these problems and must watch over myself

▲ if I fail to control myself, the society has forces that will capture and punish me

▲ my culture, and everyone's culture, is Christian and American and based on the English language, involving allegiance to all three

▲ what is normal and desirable is that some groups of people have power over other groups of people

▲ what is "abnormal" has to do, usually, with people who do not have power

▲ what happens to me personally or in my family or relationship is not to be mentioned here

▲ I will have a family and a long-term male/female relationship

▲ the useful knowledge of the world has to do with physics, chemistry, and math; and with "English" only so far as it is a "tool of communication"

▲ we live in a melting-pot society where everyone just needs to learn to get along with everyone else

This picture of what we learn in the hidden curriculum includes things we all may agree are horrible, things that may seem good to many of us, and things we can't decide about. Some items of the above list may not ring true to all of us, and many items could be added—twelve years is a long time to be in school. What is more important to acknowledge is what young people experience simply by being in a room, one that we are about to enter.

Teaching liberation

An alternative approach to teaching is crucial when the subject is sexism, racism, adultism, or violence of other kinds. Young people have experienced all of these, and know more or less perfectly well what abuse is about. Our work here is to begin with their experiences, draw these out, examine them, and uncover underlying social realities which bring them about as a first step to changing them.

With this analysis in hand, the participants themselves can begin to take charge, figuring out for themselves and each other how to stop abuse. And because this work is personal, real-life, and involves analysis and group process, the room and the teachers will look different.

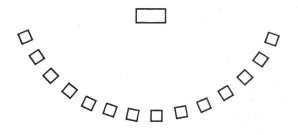

Facilitation

Facilitation means "to make easy." In this workshop, the facilitators' purpose is to bring the group along, making room for everyone to participate in a beginning-to-end process. In this context, facilitators learn as well as teach. Moreover, two facilitators working together can watch out for each other, share the tasks, and model the cooperative relationships we want young people to develop. This is particularly effective where there is a difference of age, ethnicity, race, sexual orientation, or gender between the facilitators, and that difference (if it is safe) is acknowledged and valued.

The room

Placing the chairs in a semicircle where everyone can make eye contact with everyone else brings the group itself into prominence and makes it much more possible for young people to interact with each other—a crucial part of the teaching. It can also work to have teens sit on the floor, or on top of their desks, or to simply move their chairs around the room to make themselves comfortable. In fact, what they may do is move into clusters close to their friends, which can allow them to feel safer about participating. Changing the room also adds to the informality of the group climate.

The icebreaker

"Icebreakers" is our name for group games or warm-up exercises, even songs or other music, that will further promote informality and a relaxed group climate. The usual classroom norms for youth are quite strict, if often unspoken: you have to be in a seat, sit still, no laughing, no playing, no physical contact. This is, after all, how "serious" adults are supposed to behave. But often these guidelines can prohibit or inhibit us from listening to and learning from one another, and especially from seeing one another differently. In effect they reflect the power/nonpower structure right in the human body! What we are gathered to talk about is serious enough, without adding in heavy-laden "adult" behavior.

In a single class period and in a confined classroom setting there may not be time or space to do a group game. But in virtually all other workshop settings icebreakers are important to use with young people and (even especially) with adults, both at the outset and periodically throughout the process. An icebreaker may be as minimal as everyone standing in place and stretching, as maximal as musical chairs. Consult any of the "new games" and "theater games" books for possibilities—or ask young people you work with what games they play.

The agreements

The next step is to make some agreements (see page 9), to promote group safety right at the outset. This further alters some of the traditional setting, by having the group take some charge of itself, and enabling its members (including the facilitators) to make a commitment to respect one another and participate. In essence, when a group makes and keeps agreements like confidentiality, I-statements, and no put-downs, it is modeling the just and reciprocal relationships across lines of gender, race, and age that we are trying to build.

The hand signal

One final agreement to make with the group is the hand signal. At certain arranged points in the workshop (for example, the dyad) a number of people may be speaking at once. To restore silence and attention in the group without yelling "Quiet!" a facilitator will raise her hand; when participants see the raised hand, they (a) stop talking, and (b) raise their hands. This is another way in which group members help each other to take responsibility for the process.

The dyad

A dyad is two people who talk to each other, one at a time, about what they are thinking or feeling.

In a group process where emotional issues are up for discussion, there are moments when everyone in the group will have things to say, even those who never talk in the group. It is at those moments we have everyone break into dyads, timing them so that each person in the dyad gets 2–3 minutes to talk to her/his partner about what is up. The talker uses I-statements; the listener pays attention without indulging in crosstalk or piggy-backing. Both agree not to break confidentiality later by telling someone else what was said. If the talker runs out of things to say, the listener is allowed to encourage her (him) to talk some more, or repeat what she said, or just to stay silent and notice how she is feeling. This fosters personal interaction in the group, allows every participant to get some attention, enables people who never speak with each other to do so, and makes room for non-talkers to talk. (Facilitators can also use this time to think about what to do next in the group—or about what they are feeling.)

Of course, the dyad is, by the usual social standards, a very unusual way to communicate. Few of us are trained to listen well to someone talk about what they are feeling without immediately interrupting to talk about how we are feeling or trying to give advice or trying to solve the other's problems; next to none of us has the regular experience of having someone pay complete attention to us. So it is appropriate to have everyone practice a dyad with each other at the outset, modeling for them how to listen and some ways not to listen. Here again, the time limit of a single class period may prohibit use of the dyad, but it is an essential building block for longer workshops.

The roleplays

The educator Freire worked with his adult pupils by starting with the participants' real-life situations, making them the core of the work. What makes an experience a "life situation" is the way it captures or expresses a larger theme in the participants' lives. The life situations we explore involve conflicts people really face when power is being abused. When analyzed, it can be seen that the conflict is based in a power imbalance kept in place in the society in which the participants live. We construct a roleplay to express this life situation. For example, the father-son roleplay in our curriculum depicts a father berating his son for not being "man enough." The scene is a personal one which many sons experience; the theme is the abusive socialization of boys to be men.

In our workshops we roleplay short dramatic scenes which teens can identify with, using facilitators or teens themselves to enact the parts. The process works somewhat as follows:

Stage 1. Present the roleplay—the life situation—that workshop participants actually face. Part of this process may include facilitators or participants acknowledging their personal experiences of this life situation and how it affected and affects them.

Stage 2. Facilitate the group in unraveling the scene, identifying the conflict (the abuse) and thinking out loud about the possibilities for changing the outcome of the roleplay.

Stage 3. Facilitate the group in discovering an underlying structure that sets the stage for the conflict to occur, and the theme behind the structure.

Stage 4. Conduct a group discussion in which facilitators and participants together problem-solve, strategize, and learn from each other how to change.

Stage 5. Facilitate participants' acknowledging and claiming the power they have to change situations of abuse, and their starting to make commitments of mutual support and empowerment to each other to stop the oppressive forms of power that have been passed on to them.

Using the roleplays and exercises in our curriculum, a presentation can be schematized as follows.

Male socialization roleplay

Stage 1. The life situation: a father-son roleplay

Adult   Young person

Stage 2. Discuss and unravel what happened: why is this situation happening?

Stage 3. The underlying structure: the "Act-Like-A-Man" Box

Underlying theme: male socialization.

Female socialization roleplay

Stage 1. The life situation: the party.

Men   *Women*

Stage 2. Discuss and unravel what happened: why is this situation happening?

Stage 3. The underlying structure: the "Act-Like-A-Lady" Flower.

Underlying theme: female socialization.

Cycle of oppression roleplay

Stage 1. The life situation: the power shuffle.

Persons in power   *Persons not in power*

Stage 2. Discuss and unravel the feelings about doing the exercise.

Stage 3. The underlying structure: see the power chart.

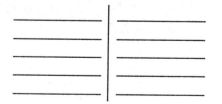

Underlying theme: oppression.

So far, we have been identifying conflicts and the underlying themes they express (stages 1–3). Now it's time to go on to intervene in and prevent the conflicts (stages 4–5).

Intervening in oppression roleplay

Stage 1. The life situation: after school.

Boyfriend   *Girlfriend*

Stages 2–3. Unravel and discuss the situation and its underlying structure: how does the boyfriend act according to the Act-Like-A-Man Box? How does the Act-Like-A-Lady Flower affect what the girlfriend does?

Stage 4. What can be done about this situation?
a. Roleplay all teen men in the class talking to and confronting the boyfriend.
   Group discussion: what went well and what got hard?

b. Roleplay all teen women in the class talking to and supporting the girlfriend.
   Group discussion: what went well and what got hard?

Stage 5. Teens taking power.
   Group discussion: what's your next step in stopping dating violence on your campus? In your life?

In closing

Beyond the roleplay, beyond the successful class, beyond the support group, and beyond the trained peer group, this educational process pictures adults and young people—men and women of very different ages, racial backgrounds, sexual orientations, and phy-

Unity Photo: Bernice Wuethrich ©1992

sical and mental abilities—finding common cause, common language, and a common understanding to face up to the very real conditions that limit us all. The solutions each group finds for its life conditions will be different. A process that works well will promote that group making its own solution and making it work. A process that works brilliantly will empower that group to reach out to educate other groups, under the ongoing principle that the teachers learn and the learners teach. This is a picture of liberation at work.

GOALS AND PROCESS FOR WORKSHOPS
by Paul Kivel

Goal # 1. Empower each individual present

Assumptions:

1. Each person's choice of attitudes, actions, and values is made as the best perceived survival strategy at the time.

2. Empowering individuals is *partly* a process of healing previous pain, hurt, and disempowerment.

3. Attitudes held with emotional intensity need to be worked through emotionally to be changed. Information alone does not change attitudes.

4. Individual growth and empowerment come from an individual's ability to combine information and past and present experience into a conscious, emotional, and intellectual process of change.

5. Empowerment happens best and is maintained most strongly with group support.

6. People become empowered through active participation.

7. Seeds of change can lie dormant for a long time.

Goal # 2. Encourage each person to be more active and involved

Assumptions:

1. An individual's personal empowerment comes through involvement in community activity.

2. Individual growth without community activity is inherently limited and is of little value to the community.

3. Powerlessness is reflected in inactivity, apathy, and cynicism.

4. Community activity breaks down isolation, self-blame, guilt,

misinformation, and extreme individualism—all of which are factors in powerlessness.

5. Community activity helps people learn about the systems of power which personally disempower us.

6. Community activity is not necessarily organized, formal, regular, or traditional. Each person can and must define her or his own way to be active.

Goal # 3. Create group solidarity, support networks, and an understanding of connection

Assumptions:

1. We are all connected.

2. We are disempowered by believing ourselves separate, fearing others, and not cooperating.

3. Our greatest resources are in our own community.

4. In any group of people, there is tremendous power to unleash. Each group already has the information and experience it needs to empower itself and its members.

5. Individual empowerment happens most easily and effectively when supported and nurtured by group energy and action.

6. Group energy snowballs to people outside the group.

Process

1. Model strength, openness, respect, trust, love, and cooperation.

2. Encourage and support openness and growth.

3. Provide information.

4. Respect the intelligence of everyone at all times.

5. Help each person identify personal issues and solutions to problems.

6. Provide a framework to aid in personal problem-solving.

7. Provide lots of options and encourage the creation of new options for problem-solving.

8. Do not try to force change on anyone.

9. Prevent people from trashing one another.

10. Emphasize that being rude, lecturing others, having an attitude of disrespect, or believing you have the "correct" information or the "correct" politics are all nonempowering attitudes.

11. Encourage and stress the importance of taking small steps toward effectively dealing with issues and participating in activities pertinent to those issues.

12. Acknowledge that people are already doing a lot of work to improve themselves and their communities.

13. As an outsider to any particular group, focus attention, facilitate discussions of people's experiences of power, share information, and focus on group self-consciousness.

14. Refer the group back to its own resources.

15. Emphasize that the group obtain information and services through nonprofessional sources and networks that already exist.

16. In most general situations, and in some specific aspects of all situations, emphasize that there are some common issues.

17. Help break down the insularity of family and relationship concepts which prevent community intervention.

18. Model and practice community intervention—friends and family reaching out to each other.

19. Talk from the heart.

Myths and Facts:
One Method That Doesn't Work
by Paul Kivel

There is a common process of public speaking and public education which relies on a technique I will call "myths and facts." It is used in the rape crisis and domestic violence movements, which is the area I work in, so I will draw examples from this area. However, its use is very widespread outside these areas as well.

This method of education has several variations, one of which goes like this. The facilitator asks the participants to describe what characters they would expect if they saw a newspaper headline which read, "Man Rapes Woman." Who would she be? Who would he be? A list of adjectives is generated; these words are supposed to represent the stereotypes. Then the facilitator systematically goes through them and explains that they are "myths" meant to confuse us; s/he then presents the "facts" about the rapist and the survivor. Sometimes the myths are presented by the facilitator as commonly held beliefs and then demolished or corrected with the facts. There is more audience participation in the former method, although it becomes a setup because all the audience answers are "incorrect" and subsequently corrected by the facilitator. This leaves the group feeling like it must rely on "experts" like the facilitator, because their own efforts to understand are so wrong.

In any case, a couple or many myths are examined and corrected, leaving the audience with more accurate information about the situations or issues under discussion. Sometimes a fact sheet is handed out to everyone so they can refer back to it after the presentation.

This method of teaching, although popular, has several serious problems. First, it immediately makes the participants wrong and the facilitator right and the expert. Second, it assumes that misinformation is the root of people's poor choices and experiences of being abused, and that giving people new information will allow them to make changes, ignoring the emotions and structures that hold their beliefs in place. Third, this method makes it difficult to connect the scattered myths into a coherent analysis—to show, for example, how sexism and racism don't exist in isolation but are part of a social framework of power and violence. Finally the use of myths and facts can mask the racism of the facilitators and make it difficult to deal with such complex issues as sexual violence and racism in effective ways.

An example of this method in a rape prevention workshop might be that the audience would say that the woman who was raped was young, dressed in a sexy way, and maybe hitchhiking. The presenter would then talk about the wide age range of rape survivors, e.g., from 3 years old to 94 years old; the variety of situations they are raped in; and the varieties of dress and activities involved in these situations. Then the presenter would move on to the next "myth."

Although this example seems simple enough, in fact it is a complicated piece of information filled with emotional as well as factual content. Let's look at the assumption behind this way of teaching, and then explore the complexities of a couple of commonly used "myths."

Basically, I understand a major underlying assumption of this method to be that people are either terribly misinformed and/or ignorant and that just giving them the "right" information will enable them to make reasonable choices about difficult situations. To some extent this is true. Our society mystifies and falsifies much of the information we get, and we certainly need more and better information so that we can make more informed choices. However, we are not perfectly reasonable, rational people. We make decisions based on our experience, other people's experiences, our knowledge, our estimation of the danger, our sense of the options and their results, and various personal and cultural characteristics. Furthermore, we take in, believe, sort through, and reuse information based on all the above named factors. Let me use an example:

Myth: Most rapists are black males and/or most black men are potentially rapists.

Fact: Most rapes occur within racial groups, i.e., white men usually rape white women, and the only reason black men are tried and convicted more often of rape is because of the racism in the legal system.

This is a common myth perpetuated in the media and in everyday racist culture. It is implicit and explicit throughout our society. We have learned it, though, not simply as a piece of wrong information. We have learned it, as we have learned all racism, as part of the emotionally laden, experientially charged fabric of our lives. As part of the training we have had as non-African-American people to grow up, live in, and maintain the system of racial power. Or as part of the training we have had as African-Americans to belittle, undervalue, and mistrust ourselves and each other.

My belief that African-American men are rapists is not just misinformation. It is information I learned at great hurt and cost while growing up, from the people I loved and trusted—my mother and father, my friends, relatives, etc. Also, this information affects me very differently if I am white than if I am African-American or of another racial background.

If I am white, then the information and its implications (i.e., that there are people I must fear, that there are people I can't be friends with, that I need to have fears around their sexuality, that there are certain people, i.e., white women, who need protection) were unwanted, resisted, and ultimately forced on me. It seemed that I had no choice but to accept the information in order to survive.

So, someone may come along today and tell me that African-American men are not rapists. I may believe them. But that may in no way affect how I feel when I next walk down a street and an African-American man approaches. For me to accept new information and for it to affect me there has to be an emotional shift in all the beliefs and experiences which connect to that one. The shift can only occur when I can release my fear and reopen my heart. Beliefs are emotionally laden, and we cannot change them without a process for working through their emotional content. If I don't, I will probably still be afraid of African-American men, but now perhaps also feel guilt and self-blame about being afraid, because I "know" they are not rapists. This confusion may, in fact, make it even more difficult for me to make useful, appropriate decisions in potentially unsafe situations.

A good alternative to just giving me new information would be to explore with me how I have learned a whole set of information about African-Americans, and African-American men in particular. Where and when and from whom did I learn it? How has it hurt me, whatever my racial heritage? How is it used to oppress us all? What fears are attached to letting go of these beliefs, and how can I get support for continuing to work on this after the facilitator leaves?

There are specific techniques for helping a group to explore these questions. The important thing is, without some process which addresses the need to explore these aspects of the "information," new facts are not going to help me change. I can use the information to tell other people they are wrong or tell myself that I am wrong because you as a facilitator said so. And you have become one more authority in my life telling me what to believe or not to believe—not an ally helping me be more powerful and less willing to pass on racial violence in the guise of protecting myself.

Even more serious questions are raised about the "myth/fact" approach when this myth represents the only way that racism is dealt with in a presentation. This, in fact, may be the main reference to racism in a workshop on sexual violence. Although it is clearly inadequate as a method for addressing racism in a workshop, I have heard this myth/fact exercise justified because "we have to deal with racism." Covering this myth does not deal with racism. Individual beliefs about race do not even constitute racism. Individual beliefs about race are the result of the institutionalized oppression and violation of one people by another based on race. Since, in our society, this provides the context for our entire lives and belief systems, dealing with racism involves examining that context, healing the pain and hurt, correcting the misinformation, setting a process in motion to continue dealing with racism, and acting to challenge the system of institutionalized violence itself in a community of people. Parts of each of these tasks can and need to be incorporated into every workshop intentionally and effectively.

Here is another standard example:

Myth: The man to fear is a stranger.

Fact: A woman or child is most likely to experience sexual or physical violence from someone they have known intimately and trusted such as a husband, father, stepfather, friend, or relation.

This is earthshaking news indeed—not something to toss out as part of a section on protecting oneself. If we are allowed to explore this "fact" together honestly and deeply, we may learn why we don't already know it, or that we do but can't acknowledge it. We would have to process how we personally have been hurt by those we love, how our concept of love itself is bound up with violence, and how we might have to reevaluate and shift our entire perception of people in order to accept this "information." And depending on who we are, where we live, and other factors, it may or may not be true for you or me. The implications of this terrible "fact," that I should fear and protect myself from those I love and who love me, carries assumptions we must examine together and that we can't take casually out of context.

The myth/fact presentation also makes it appear that these two myths are unrelated and that sexism and racism are separate issues. It seems clear, however, that male violence against women and children in families is protected and hidden by training us (both whites and people of color) to look at people of color as dangerous and violent. We are taught that the danger is "out there," in "them," and that we need our fathers and other white men to protect us. It is extremely difficult to challenge your abuser if you believe that you need his protection because there are even worse dangers outside.

I have heard each of these myths presented, built up, and then demolished in 5 or 10 minutes. I have seen people told that they are wrong for believing the myths. I have seen people become confused, upset, disbelieving and frustrated, and made to feel inadequate or stupid because they couldn't just throw out their life's learning and experience and accept a few simple new pieces of information. But they could figure out well enough what the facilitator wanted to hear. And, on a posttest, they could give the right answers.

Why is it that we want to believe that this methodology works? I can offer some suggestions. We as educators often have a certain desperation about getting the message out, affecting people, helping them, protecting them. We believe that it is dangerous out there and this work will make it safer. Whether we have 15 minutes at a luncheon talk, or three hours at a workshop, there is always more to say, do, and pass on to people than we have time for. We each want to feel powerful and effective in our lives and in our work. We want to feel that we make a difference. We also see people as victims of violence, unprotected, needing our help, relying on us to guide them through.

These are all our own emotional needs and not the needs of those with whom we talk. We need to get support, appreciation, feedback, etc., from each other, as co-workers, so that we don't implicitly set up our methodology to meet our own needs for reassurance, calming, hope, and support as teachers, workers, and adults.

Our theories of violence also tend to reinforce this methodology. We speak of victims of violence. We talk of women or children as victims, as needing defense against violence. We begin to see our task as helping to protect women, making them less vulnerable to dangerous situations, giving them the advice they need to feel or be safer. And the world gets divided up into men who are abusers and women who are abused. In this model, women need self-defense classes and safety advice. Now, all women and children and men could use self-defense training and safety advice, but there are reasons why it isn't taught, and reasons why, once we know it, we don't necessarily use it. In the complex reality in which we live, where we move into and out of relationships with a constantly shifting dynamic of power, no one is a perpetual victim or abuser. We have all experienced and internalized the powerlessness of this society. We have all survived the violence in our lives. We have all learned to pass on our powerlessness and hurt by passing on hurt and violence to ourselves and those around us. A man violated on the job may abuse his female partner. A heterosexual person of color, violated by white society, may violate gay and lesbian people. A woman violated by her boss, co-worker, or husband may violate her kids, or her students. And any of us may violate ourselves through drugs, "accidents" actually caused by overwork or stress, and not taking care of ourselves properly.

We need theories which understand not only the external oppression but the ways we have internalized and gone along with that oppression, both by recreating and responding to violence. We need methods which draw on our experiences and our strength as survivors to come together and challenge the values and expectations underlying our society. No one of us is simply a victim. We are all complex players and survivors in a system which tries to destroy us and keep us apart. As facilitators, it is crucial that we acknowledge our own roles and experiences in this society and acknowledge the strength, experience, and concern which absolutely every person brings to our workshops.

A final and important reason we stay with this inappropriate myth/facts methodology is because it is safe for us as facilitators. We have all the information, all the facts. We no longer believe the myths and are cured of the diseases of sexism, or racism, or whatever. We don't have to be open or vulnerable. We don't have to deal with other people's difficult experiences. We don't have to risk ourselves. All we really have to do is to have our facts correct and give entertaining presentations so that people will absorb the information and take it home with them. We don't have to love, or care about, or even necessarily respect the people we are talking with, and we don't have to feel any common bonds. In fact, we don't have to feel much at all. This is, after all, just an exchange of information—the debunking of myths.

Our lives are hard, our work situations difficult at best. This particular kind of work is poorly rewarded, and all of us have been hurt by the violence of our society. Most of us have never been given a chance to work through our personal issues and heal from our painful experiences. We don't always feel powerful enough in this work: powerful enough to risk our lives, powerful enough to trust the people in our workshops, powerful enough to open ourselves up to others in our work. Because of this sense of powerlessness, we stick with safe techniques which keep us in control, feeling powerful and effective and separate. But by staying in control, we ultimately end up feeling more powerless, because people invariably don't make the changes we want them to. We remain isolated and our work is ineffective in building genuine community responses to end the violence.

When our needs for support are being met elsewhere, when we can acknowledge our common bonds and struggles with the people with whom we are speaking, when we love and respect them and understand the complexity of our common situation, and when we can let go of our need for control and personal safety—only then can we take the time to listen to whom we are speaking, and make room for their questions, concerns, experiences, and knowledge to become the framework for our work. Our effectiveness can then be measured in the empowerment of the participants, not in the amount of discon-nected information we transfer to them. And the myth that this methodology of "myths and facts" works will be just that, another myth, and not a fact of our work together.

Section 4

High School Program

Photo: Francisco Garcia ©1992

This section is the workhorse—what we actually do in the classroom. We begin with a "Before the Class" checklist for facilitators. Then we outline possible one-day (one class-period of 45–50 minutes), two-day, and three-day agendas. The three-day agenda uses the BWA video, *My Girl*. Note the highly recommended alternative two-day outline on page 83, which weaves in related issues of racism, adultism, and other kinds of power imbalances.

The in-depth two-day script, addressing family and relationship violence and sex-role socialization, takes you through the curriculum step by step. This is where you will find each exercise explained in detail.

1. Talk with the teacher ahead of time to determine what the age, gender, and racial composition of the class is; what the teacher expects, what the students expect and any general information relevant to your presentation (e.g., any recent incident of violence at the school.)

2. In this contact, or in a brief meeting with the teacher just before class begins, let the teacher know what you expect from her or him, find out how much time you will have, and whether the teacher has any special needs. Ask to be able to introduce yourself, rather than having the teacher do it. Find out exactly when class ends and whether there will be intercom announcements at the beginning or end of class. Be sure there will be chalk, a chalkboard, etc., available to you.

3. Meet with your co-presenter; set up the agenda and decide who does what. Gather the forms and materials you will need.

4. Meet with your co-presenter at the classroom a few minutes before the program to check in, make any last minute changes, and set up video equipment, if needed.

5. Make verbal contact with the teacher and at least eye contact with class members as they come in. Introduce yourself informally.

6. Look over the classroom and set it up as you want it. You may want the teacher and teens to arrange chairs in a semi-circle, or perhaps have them sit on top of their desks, or otherwise arrange themselves to encourage intimacy and informality.

7. Go to it; have a ball!

HIGH SCHOOL PROGRAM OUTLINES

One-day high school presentation outline

1. Introduction and Agreements
2. Act-Like-A-Man Box
3. Act-Like-A-Lady Flower
4. After School roleplay
5. Getting help, Resources
6. Wrap-up, questions, comments

Two-day high school presentation outline

Day 1

1. Introduction and Agreements
2. Father-Son roleplay
3. Act-Like-A-Man Box
4. Party roleplay
5. Writing about a personal experience of violence

Day 2

1. Review
2. One Thing
3. Act-Like-A-Lady Flower
4. Comments on personal experience of violence essays/accounts
5. Facilitator's personal experience of violence
6. After School roleplay
7. Getting help, Resources
8. Wrap-Up, questions, comments

Alternative two-day high school presentation outline

Day 1

1. Introduction and Agreements
2. Father-Son roleplay
3. Act-Like-A-Man Box
4. Party roleplay
5. One Thing/Act-Like-A-Lady Flower
6. Writing about a personal experience of violence

Day 2

1. Review
2. Power Shuffle (see page 14)
3. Power Chart (see page 16)
4. Nonpower visualization Part 1 (see page 21)
5. After School roleplay
6. Getting help, Resources
7. Wrap-up, questions, comments

Three-day high school presentation outline (with video)

Day 1

1. Introduction and Agreements

2. Father-Son roleplay
3. Act-Like-A-Man Box
4. Introduce Video: *My Girl*
   a. Explain that the video was made with student volunteers from Contra Costa County, California. Explain that personal, emotional issues might come up for them during the video, so they should get comfortable and remember that any information or feelings that come up in the discussion afterward will be kept confidential, with three exceptions (see pages 130–131).
   b. Show the first third of the video

Day 2

1. Review
2. Party roleplay
3. Act-Like-A-Lady Flower
4. Show middle section of video
5. Writing about a personal experience of violence

Day 3

1. Review and questions
2. Open discussion
3. Talk about personal experience of violence essays/accounts
4. Facilitator's personal experience of violence
5. After School roleplay
6. Show final third of video (if time)
7. Getting help, Resources
8. Wrap-Up, questions, comments

TWO-DAY HIGH SCHOOL PRESENTATION SCRIPT

Day 1

1. Introduction and Agreements

Ask the students to arrange chairs/desks in a semicircle with every student visible. Have them sit on top of the desks, if possible (see page 66).

Introduce yourselves, and your organization, if relevant. Follow with a statement, such as the one below, on stopping violence:

a. We are here to talk with you about stopping violence—the violence that men do to women in relationships and that adults do to children in families. This can be violence that is physical, like hitting; sexual, like rape and incest; or emotional, like yelling and put-downs. And we are going to talk about violence among teens, like bullying and dating violence.

b. We believe that family and teen violence are connected. Boys are not born violent, and no girl likes to be hit. But all of us are taught sex roles as children, and a lot of that "teaching" is violent. It can teach boys that you have to be tough and girls that you have to put up with what guys do.

c. We are going to spend the next two days with you talking about being raised male and being raised female and looking at the violence that comes out of that training. Then we are going to try to figure out how to stop it.

d. We want to accomplish three goals during these two days. (Write on board.) We want each of us to be able to
    1. Recognize violence
    2. Say "No" to violence
    3. Get help when needed

    Now these may seem pretty basic, but for some of us, they will be hard to do. If I have been raised in a home where my dad hits my mom, I may think it's OK to hit my girlfriend. We want you to recognize this as violence and recognize that it is not OK. About the second goal—saying "No" doesn't mean just saying the word "no." It means saying NO to violence in everything we do. And our third goal—it can be real scary sometimes to ask for help. But if you realize during this presentation that you need or want help, we want you to get help for yourself.

e. If you are in a situation in which someone is hurting you or someone else you know, we are here for you to talk to, and there are different ways you can talk to us. You can talk to us anonymously, in writing, or you can talk to us after class or by phone. If you tell us you are being hurt or have been hurt by an adult or someone older than you, we will need to get you help from others, and will make a referral to get you help. Another way we can help you is by giving you information so you can decide where and how to get help.

To conclude the introduction, go over "The Basic Agreements" (page 9), in a form something like this:

Because the kind of violence that we will be talking about today is personal, and because it has to do with how each of us learns how to be a man or a woman, we will be dealing with things that can be very hard. For that reason, we like to make a few agreements with each other before we start. First of all, we agree to keep confidentiality. That means that whatever is said in this room stays in this room. Second, we agree to listen to each other and not putdown or attack anybody. Third, we agree to acknowledge feelings and, that feelings, both, good and sad, are OK to have and OK to talk about. And finally, if you tell one of us about an abusive relationship you are in, we promise to work with you personally to get you some help to deal with it. Can everyone agree to this? OK, then let's start with a roleplay.

▲ 1. Father-Son roleplay

Presenter (**P**) plays the father (**F**), and a male student from the class is chosen to play the son (**S**). The son is sitting down watching TV (let the student pick the show) and the father enters the room waving a report card. (Prepare the student by explaining the scenario; get agreement on physical contact.)

F: Turn off the TV! What the hell are you doing? And what the hell is this? (Shows report card.)

S: It's my report card.

F: Your report card! If you're so smart, why were you stupid enough to get a D in Math?

S: I did the best I could.

F: D is the best you could do? You're just stupid!

S: That's not fair. (Tries to get up.)

F: (Shoves him down.) Don't you talk back to me! You hear, boy?

S: (Starts to cry.)

F: Oh, you gonna cry now? Huh? (Shakes son, hits him with report card.) You can't even act like a man! (Stomps out. Son stops in place to end the roleplay.)

P asks the son: How are you feeling right now about yourself? About your father? About what just happened?

P asks the class: What's going on here? Why is this fight happening? Who is responsible? Is this really about grades?

P: One thing the father told his son is to "act like a man." Let's talk about that.

▲ 2. The "Act-Like-A-Man" Box

P talks to teen men in the room, who pretend for a moment that they are 10 years old and that there is an adult man—father, stepfather, coach, etc.—who is angrily saying to them, "Act like a man." **P** says this in an angry, yelling tone to each of them, and then steps back from that role.

P: What are you guys learning when someone says that to you?

Co-presenter writes a list on the board of the characteristics the students name. Be sure to include "tough" and its equivalents, and "don't cry." Draw a box around the entire list and label it "Act-Like-A-Man" (see page 88).

(A note on "macho": Invariably someone will mention "macho" as a male characteristic. Always suggest an English term instead, and take a minute to explain that "macho" is a Spanish/Mexican term, having to do with honor, taking care of one's family, etc., that has been misused negatively in English as "tough, insensitive," and then reapplied to Mexican men as a stereotype. To avoid this form of racism, it is best not to use the term at all.)

P: We call this our "Act-Like-A-Man" box. We believe that all boys learn about this box as they grow up. Who are some of the people in society that teach us to be this way?

(**Co-P** lists: parents, friends, lovers, media, coaches, teachers, grandparents.)

P: What names do boys get called when they try to step outside of this box?

(**Co-P** writes the names along the right side of the box.)

P: What is the purpose of these names? What are you supposed to do when someone calls you these names?

P: What is the particular purpose of *these* names? (Point out the names "fag," "queer," and any others that refer to gays.) When boys hear them, what are they being taught about being close to other boys or men? What are they being told about gay men? How does this fear of being labeled keep men in the box?

(Note: be prepared to address misinformation about gay people and the anxiety that will bubble right up when you even refer to this subject.)

P: These names are little slaps in the face, telling us to get back in the box. They are emotionally violent, they hurt us, and they make us want to change our behavior so we never get called these names again.

P: What happens to boys physically? How do they get treated physically to make sure they act like men? (**Co-P** writes down list on other side of box, and then draws a fist around either side of the box.)

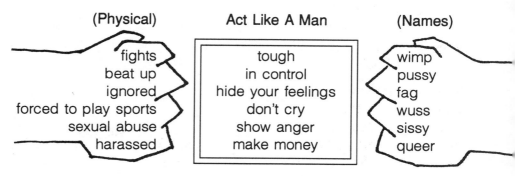

(Physical)   Act Like A Man   (Names)

fights	tough	wimp
beat up	in control	pussy
ignored	hide your feelings	fag
forced to play sports	don't cry	wuss
sexual abuse	show anger	sissy
harassed	make money	queer

P: Something else that happens to boys besides getting beat up is that one out of six boys is sexually abused before the age of 18. These boys are usually abused by a man, not gay, who may seem to be "like everyone else"—he may have a wife, children, etc. What is it about this box is that going to make it real hard for a guy who's been sexually abused to talk about it and get help? What names will he be called if he talks?

We're going into this because part of the message for men is: when you get hurt, take it in, keep it in, don't ever tell anyone. Now, when you raise someone from the time he is a baby to take the pain, keep it to himself, and not to show any feelings except anger, you're training someone to walk around like a time bomb. What is going to happen when this person is 17 or 18 or 20 and finds himself getting mad or upset about something?

We can see from the box that boys are not born to be violent, but that they get emotionally and physically hurt to make them stay in control. No boy wants it to be this way, and all of us as guys try to figure out how to get out of this box.

Let's talk now about being raised female. We'll start off this section with a roleplay, too.

▲ 3. Party roleplay

P picks a male and female volunteer from the class. **Scenario:** the male (**M**) and female (**F**) are boyfriend and girlfriend. They have been in a relationship for the past eight months. They have sex on a regular basis and use birth control consistently and responsibly. **F**'s best friend's parents are gone for the weekend, and so the best friend is having a party. There is beer and wine coolers and people are listening to music and dancing. **M** and **F** end up in the parents' master bedroom. They are not drunk or high.

The Male Role: M wants to have sex with **F**. He knows they do it almost every Saturday night and he wants to tonight. He loves her, but will not take "No" for an answer. Plus, his friends saw him go upstairs, and he feels he will need to tell them a good story when he goes back downstairs. Give the roleplayer permission to use every line in the book.

The Female Role: F loves **M** a lot. He is very popular, very good-looking, and a lot of other girls would love to go out with him. But, tonight she doesn't want to have sex with **M**—just because she doesn't feel like it. Plus, she feels like all of their friends are watching them and she feels self-conscious. However, she's scared of losing **M**, so she doesn't want to make him mad.

The Script: It might be easiest to begin the roleplay with **M** putting his arm around **F** and saying, "I really want to have sex with you tonight." A last line for the roleplay can be **M** saying, "Goddamit, I'm gonna get what I want from you *now!*" Let the roleplayers fill in in-between, with the focus being on **M** pressuring **F** physically and emotionally and **F** politely trying to get him to see her viewpoint. They freeze in place to end the roleplay.

P asks the boyfriend, in character: How are you feeling about what you're doing? How do you feel right now about yourself?

P asks the girlfriend, in character: How are you feeling about what your boyfriend is doing to you? What keeps you from saying these things to your boyfriend? What are you afraid of?

P then "freezes" the boyfriend, asking him to listen without reacting negatively, and has the girlfriend tell him how she feels and what she wants/needs from him.

P asks for class feedback: What do you see happening here? Is the boyfriend "acting-like-a-man?" Why is he doing what he's doing? How does she feel? Is it hard for her to say "No?" Why? What kind of violence is happening here?

P thanks the volunteers and asks the class to give them a round of applause.

P: Now, we'll finish talking about women tomorrow, so I want you to remember this roleplay we've just done. Look around at school—notice the way that men and women act around you. Do you meet guys who fit in the box? Guys who are out of the box? Think about some experiences you have had as a woman. Are any similar to our roleplay?

P may choose tell a personal experience about dating violence, if it seems appropriate.

▲ 4. Writing about a personal experience of violence

P: We have looked today at what teen women and men learn about how we as adults (if **P** is an adult) expect you and train you to act. This training hurts us all, and it's a setup for violence. The first thing we need to do to "unlearn" this training is to look at how it affects each of us. We are going to take the last 5–10 minutes of this class to write, anonymously, about how each of us has been touched by violence. (Pass out the form; adapt the sample on page 136 to your needs.)

Make yourself comfortable, spread out so you don't have people looking at your paper, think about a time when you were hurt or made to feel afraid, and write to us about it. Take your time, and pay attention to how you feel. We have you do these writings for several reasons. First, because writing about an experience where you have been hurt is sometimes the first, and possibly easiest, step toward dealing with what has happened to you. Second, these writings will help us focus on what to talk about with you tomorrow. Finally, these writings help us learn what is really going on at your school and in young people's lives.

If you would like to talk to one of us about your experience, so that we can get you help, you may put your name on your paper and we will contact you, *not* at home, and help you deal with what's going on in your life. However, these are anonymous and you do *not* need to put your name on this paper. We will not show anyone these papers—not even your teacher. When you are through writing, please put the papers face down on the table.

P: (after writings are collected) Thanks—we'll see you tomorrow.

Day 2 (Also note alternative two-day outline, page 83)

1. Review

Presenters reintroduce themselves and review the first day with help from the students.

P: Yesterday we looked at what boys learn about being men and how that "learning" hurts us. We saw two violent or nearly violent roleplays—a father yelling at his son and a guy pressuring his girlfriend for sex—and we saw how these train boys to "act like men." We started looking at being raised female by talking about what was happening in the party roleplay. Now I want us to think back to that roleplay and what happened with the boyfriend and what happened with the girlfriend. I want us to talk about what this roleplay and society as a whole tell us about how women are "supposed to act."

▲ 1. One Thing

P: (to the women in the class) What is one thing that men or boys say to you—something that hurts you or that you don't like—that you never want to hear again. You can think back to the roleplay and some lines the boyfriend used on the girlfriend. (**Co-P** writes the comments off to one side of the board.)

One Thing

trust me
if you loved me you would
I'll call you
you'll do what I tell you
you're my woman
no fat chicks allowed

▲ 2. Act-Like-A-Lady Flower

P: (still to the women in the class) What is this list of things men say to you telling you about how you are supposed to act as a woman? What in your upbringing have you learned about how you are supposed to act if you are a "good girl"? How does society tell you to act if you are going to act like a "lady"? (**Co-P** writes down responses about "how women are supposed to act." Expect responses such as "sexy but not too sexy," "smart but not too smart," "listener," and "caretaker.") Draw a flower around this list and label it "Act Like A Lady."

Act Like A Lady

sweet
sexy, but not too sexy
passive
listener
smart, but not too smart
caretaker

P: We call this the "Act-Like-A-Lady" Flower. Just like in the Act-Like-A-Man Box, women who are out of this flower get called names to make them stay in the flower, to make them act the way society says "nice women" should act. What are some names women get called if they step out of the flower? (**Co-P** lists on board to the right side. You will get names like whore, slut, ho, tramp, bitch, frigid, virgin, lesbo, dyke, butch.)

P: So, women get called different names for being out of the flower in different ways. Maybe if you as a woman are "too smart, "according to the flower, you'll be called a bitch. Maybe if a woman is "overly provocative," according to society, then she is called one of the "whore" words. Maybe if a woman is "too athletic" for the flower, she'll be called a dyke.

You might have noticed that a lot of the names guys get called have to do with being tough—they are about what guys *do*. What do you notice about a lot of these names? Most of them are about women being—or not being—sexual. Women are identified by how they *look*.

P: How about these particular names? (Point out "dyke," "lesbo," and other terms referring to lesbians.) What happens to women who want close relationships of any kind with other women? What message do you get about lesbians from these names? What's the purpose of these names?

(Note: Again, be prepared to deal with misinformation—and panic—about this subject in the classroom.)

P: What are some of the physical things that get done to women who step out of the flower? (**Co-P** lists these to the left. You will get answers such as: rape, hitting, job discrimination, a bad reputation, date rape, molesting, catcalls, pinches, etc.) So, now our flower looks like this:

(Physical)	Act Like A Lady	(Verbal)
rape	sweet	whore
hitting	sexy, but not too sexy	bitch
molest	passive	dyke
bad reputation	listener	frigid
catcalls/whistles	smart, but not too smart	tramp
pinched	caretaker	slut
job descrimination	polite	butch

P: We feel that it is really important to point out something about the act of rape: a woman can be raped regardless of whether she is in the flower or not, just by virtue of being a woman. A woman can be perfectly in the flower and be raped, and a woman can be totally out of the flower and be raped. It is really scary to look at this. The statistic is that one out of three or four girls is sexually abused by the time she is 18, usually by an adult man. And one out of three teen women in a dating relationship in high school gets physically or sexually abused.

P: Now that we've looked at both the flower and the box, what is it about them that leads to violence in teen relationships? (Get open discussion going with class around this question.)

4. Comments on personal experience of violence essays/accounts

P: Now we want to focus on this class in particular for a moment. First of all, we want to appreciate you. Some of the things you wrote about are very hard to deal with. Some of you wrote that you have never shared your experience before. So, we want to commend you on your bravery and honesty. We also want to encourage you to not stop here with it; get some help for yourself if you feel you need it. Maybe that means telling your best friend who you trust a lot; or maybe that means coming up to us after class; or maybe it means calling one of our crisis numbers. Whatever the way you need to take care of yourself, we encourage you to do it.

This can be the time to focus on some specific issues which came up in the writings. For instance:

P: Some of you wrote about being yelled at a lot by your parents and how that hurts, but also how you thought "it wasn't a big deal, it's just verbal abuse." We think it is a big deal if it hurts you. Many times, emotional abuse hurts as much as physical abuse, and we want you to know that you don't deserve to be abused—in any way. (You can list some specific resources on the board for this part. For example, if a student writes about contemplating suicide, you can address this directly, without pointing out the student, and write the suicide crisis number on the board.)

5. Facilitator's personal experience of violence

This can be fit in wherever it feels most comfortable and appropriate for the students and for the facilitator telling his/her experience.

▲ 6. After School roleplay

P: Now we want to work with *you* about how you can help each other to deal with relationship violence. A lot of times it's easier to talk with a friend about what is going on in your life than with an adult. Because of this, we want you to know how you can help if you know a guy who hits his girlfriend, or a girl who is in an abusive relationship, or if *you* are this girlfriend or boyfriend. We'll start with showing you a roleplay, and then we'll have you all join us in this roleplay.

Presenters play the roles of boyfriend and girlfriend. (In this roleplay unlike the previous ones, the roles are complicated, requiring both presenters.)

Scenario: The Boyfriend has been saving up his money for two years to buy a car (something cool, like a sports car or a Jeep). He bought his car last night and talked to his girlfriend, who said she'd like to go riding in it after school the next day. *But,* **the Girlfriend** just found out she's getting an F in _____ (use class you are in). Her school counselor called her parents in for a conference and said that if she finished her book report tonight and turned it in tomorrow, she could pass the class. Her parents put her on restriction—she has to go straight home.

Boyfriend (**B**) runs into girlfriend (**G**) in the hall.

B: Hey, girl, where you goin'?

G: Oh, hi! I'm so busted. I'm getting an F in _____ , and I've got to get home right now.

B: No way, you're not going home now. I got my car last night; you know, the one I've been saving up for. We're going for a ride—now!

G: Honey, I would love to, but I'm serious. I'm in big trouble. My dad's waiting for me. I've *got* to go home.

B: I don't believe this crap. You're my girl, aren't you? You do what I say. (Grabs her arm.)

G: Yes, I'm your girl, but—come on, mellow out. You're hurting me.

B: Listen, this isn't even about studying, is it? You're really going to meet Mike, aren't you? Your friends told me last period you're going out with him!

G: I am *not*! I love you. What are you talking about? (She's heard this all before.)

B: I'm sick of this. You're coming with me now! (Starts pulling her.)

G: (Tries to get away, knows what is coming.)

B: (Starts to swing.) Bitch!

Both freeze.

Talk to the Boyfriend: Presenter playing the boyfriend (**B**) stays in role. **Co-P** gets all the male students in the class to come up and form a semicircle around **B**. The semicircle should face the teen women.

> **Co-P:** (to the teen men) **P** will stay in role as the boyfriend. You all are going to roleplay that you are his friends. Some of you are his best friends—you've grown up together. Some of you work with him. Others of you play basketball with him. Some of you are friends with his girlfriend, too. You have just seen your friend hit his girlfriend. How are you going to act with him now?

B begins to interact with the teen men as his "buds," trying to get his friends to be "on his side." **B** cajoles, bad-mouths, teases, asks for his friends' support. The teen men will interact in a variety of ways. After **B** gets comments from all the teen men, he freezes and switches back to being the Presenter.

> **P:** (to rest of class) What did the "friends" do that helped to intervene in and stop the violence? (**P** pulls some responses from the class to support positive interventions teen men can do with each other.)

P: (to teen men) What does this friend of yours need from you so that he will really stop hitting his girlfriend? (**P** aims for these sorts of responses from the teen men:)

1. **B** needs to be told it's not OK to hit his girlfriend.

2. **B** needs to be told his friends care about him and will stick by him and try to help him.

3. **B** needs to be asked, "What's going on with *you*, that would make you hit your girlfriend?"

Talk to the Girlfriend: Presenter playing the girlfriend (**G**) gets back into role. **Co-P** has teen women form a semicircle around the girlfriend, facing the teen men in the room.

The setup will be the same as in talking with the boyfriend. **G** will interact with the teen women, asking them to help her. **G** should aim at getting the teen women to

1. See if she is physically OK.

2. Offer her their assistance in a variety of ways, e.g., give her a ride home, protect her from **B** as she leaves the school grounds, go out with her on the weekend, sit with her while she calls **B**, hold her hand when she tells her parents what's going on, etc.

The teen women will interact in a variety of ways. After every teen woman has had a chance to comment, **G** will freeze and go back to her role as Presenter.

P: (to the teen women) What does this friend of yours need now so that she can stay safe? (**P** aims at these responses:)

1. **G** needs to know it's not her fault and that she doesn't deserve to be hit.
2. **G** needs to be helped so that she is immediately physically safe.
3. **G** does not need to be told that her boyfriend is a jerk and that she is stupid for being/staying with him. **G** needs to be listened to, not given advice.
4. **G** needs to be told that her friends will be there for her to talk with, spend time with, so that she doesn't have to be dependent on her boyfriend.

Finally, roleplayer **G** and several women friends continue the roleplay: they safely walk **G** past **B** to the parking lot. The friends figure out with each other how to handle getting past **B** and then do it. **B** should be prepared to "give in" to them, not prolonging the roleplay.

P thanks both groups for roleplaying and does a quick wrap-up about what was just said.

7. Getting help, Resources

P: Getting help from friends to deal with and prevent violence is important. Who in your life now could you get help from to deal with abuse? Beyond immediate contacts, who can you get help from? (**P** describes local services, and passes out crisis cards or xeroxed list.)

P: This lists crisis numbers and numbers for lots of places you can call to get help. You don't have to give your name. You can call even if you just have a question about what this service does. And you can slip this to a friend who might need some help.

All of us are affected by violence some time in our lives, particularly as young people and as women. We each have the right to recognize when it's happening, say no to it, get help, and help each other to stop it.

8. Wrap-up, questions, comments

Field any remaining questions or observations from the group in the time that's left. Be sure to thank the class and end on a positive note.

Section 5

Workshops

Unity Photo: Laraine Wing ©1992

This section offers suggested outlines for separate 4- to 6-hour work-shops that focus on unlearning adultism, sexism, and racism. They are truly suggestions, based on what we have tried with youth, adult and combined youth/adult groups over the years. Use them as a springboard.

As in all presentations, cofacilitation is crucial. Facilitators' diversity in age, race, gender, sexual orientation, and so forth always increases the power of the workshop; trained youth facilitators exponentially compound it. And it is important, as you develop your presentations, to allow lots of process time for mutual support for preparation before and debriefing after them. You, too, get to have safety, healing, liberation, and justice in this work.

A Workshop on Teen Oppression and Unlearning Adultism

We have worked with many adults and young people on the issue of adultism. We have found that this oppression causes much pain and anger for young people and a barrier to closeness for adults who interact with young people, either professionally or personally. We have devised this workshop as a way of breaking down the walls which adultism forms between adults and young people. This workshop will work best with a mixed group of 20–40 adults and young people, but it can also work with a small number of adults (as part of a training for teens).

Sample agenda (time: 4 hours)

1. Opening Exercise: Teen Poster Exercise
   As participants walk in, they begin the Teen Poster Exercise. Posters are hung along the wall, labeled with the ages 11–18, one age on each poster. Participants write down significant events that happened to them at these specific ages. (An alternate to this exercise is a group icebreaker.)

2. Introductions and Agreements
   Practice dyad (see page 67)

3. Being a Teenager
   a. Teen Visualization
   Facilitator: Pick an age when you were a teen—the first one that pops in your head.
   - What do people call you? What are your nicknames?
   - Where do you go to school? What does your school look like? What is it like between classes when everyone's in the halls?
   - What are you wearing? What are your favorite clothes? What does your hair look like?
   - What music are you listening to?
   - Who are your best friends? What do they look like? Talk like?
   - Where do you live? What does your house/apartment look like? Who lives there? When you walk in, where is the first place you go? The safest place? The place you might avoid?

   b. Break into dyads to talk about experience as a teen.

c. Group process: What came up for everyone?

4. Teen Oppression
   a. Stand-Up exercise on the experience of being limited by an adult (use Adultism Visualization and Teens Stand-Up, pages 56–57). Break into dyads.
   b. Group discussion
   c. Statement on what the adultism is and the role of adults as allies
   d. Ask for questions

5. Separate Age-Group Discussion
   Group breaks into teen and adult sub-groups. Suggested discussion questions:

Teens	Adults
What I need adults to know about us	Expectations I learned about the adult role
What I never want to hear from adults again	What this tells me about myself
What I expect from adults as my allies	What I need from other adults in order to listen well to young people
	My next steps for being an ally to young people

(30–45 minutes)

6. Teens Speak-Out
   a. Explain the Speak-Out (nonpower group talks, power group listens and then repeats back what they heard)
   b. Teens, linking arms, facing adults as a group, answer above "teen" questions (10 minutes)
   c. After they finish, adults respond, "I heard you say—" repeating word for word what the teens said without editing, editorializing, or adding to the teens' statements (5 minutes)

7. Closing
   a. Getting help, Resources
   b. Statement on building alliances
   c. Appreciations

A Workshop on Unlearning Sexism

Much of this agenda is duplicated in our high school presentation script. Please refer to those scripts and roleplays while reading this agenda. This workshop focuses on learning about sex-role conditioning and the role that our conditioning plays in male violence toward, and oppression of, women. This workshop will work best when the ratio of men to women is equal.

Sample agenda (time: 4 hours)

1. Icebreaker, introduction, agreements, practice dyad

2. Growing up male and female. Context setting:
   a. Growing up male
      ▲ Father-Son roleplay
      ▲ Act-Like-a-Man Box
   b. Growing up female
      ▲ Party roleplay
      ▲ One thing/Act-Like-a-Lady Flower
   c. Stand-Up exercises
      ▲ Men Stand-Up exercise (see page 26)
      ▲ Women Stand-Up exercise (see page 27)
      ▲ Break into dyads with member of the same gender on what feelings came up during these exercises

3. Women's group/Men's group. Suggested discussion questions:

Women's group	Men's group
Experience of being hurt by a man	Experience of being hurt by an adult man/trained by an adult man to "act like a man"
What keeps me from getting close to other women	What I am proud of about being a man
What I need from other women	What might keep me from listening to women speak out
	My next step in listening well to women

4. Speak-Out
  a. Explain the Speak-Out
  b. Women speak-out to men (10 minutes):
    ▲ What I want you to know about us is _____
    ▲ One thing I never want to see, hear from, or have done by a man again is _____
    ▲ What I expect from men as my allies is _____
    ▲ After listening to all of the women's statements, men, supporting each other, say "I heard you say—" and repeat word for word what the women said without editing, editorializing, or adding (5 minutes)

5. Closing
  a. Getting help, Resources
  b. Statement on building alliances
  c. Appreciations

A Workshop on Unlearning Racism

Note: This workshop focuses on looking at power imbalances and alliances across racial and cultural lines. The conclusion of this agenda includes a Speak-Out, with the people of color in the group speaking out against the oppression done to them by white people. This will only work if the number of people of color in the group is large enough to ensure their safety in speaking out about this issue. As in all the workshops, multicultural, highly skilled facilitation is essential to making the workshop a success.

Sample agenda (time: 4 hours)

1. Context setting: Power
  a. Power Shuffle
  b. Dyads (see page 67)
  c. Power Chart
  d. Nonpower visualization (see pages 21–22)

2. Definitions. Facilitators discuss the following topics (see "Racism," page 32). Then group breaks into pairs to discuss
  a. Racism—systematic mistreatment
  b. No reverse racism
  c. Internalized oppression
  d. How we "learn" oppressive attitudes long before we experi-

ence individual incidents which might appear to justify the attitudes

    e. Conditioning of whites

    f. The role of white people as allies

3. Whites and People of Color Stand-Ups (or this can be included in #4)

4. Separate groups. Suggested discussion questions:

People of Color	Whites
Pride in my ethnicity	Pride in my ethnicity
One way my people have been hurt by racism	Early experience of hearing that people of color were different
One thing I'm afraid is true about what they say about my people	My next step in being closer to people of color in my life
What I need/expect from my white allies	What might keep me from listening well to people of color

5. Speak-Out
People of color speak out to whites answering the following questions:
    ▲ What I want you to know about my people
    ▲ What I never want to hear or have done to me by whites again
    ▲ What I expect from my white allies (10 minutes)

Whites, supporting each other reply, "I heard you say—." They repeat word for word what the people of color said, without editing, editorializing, or adding (5 minutes)

6. Closing
    a. Getting help, Resources
    b. Statement on welcoming difference
    c. Group hug and appreciations

Section 6

Support Groups

After the class, what's next? One direction is youth empowerment, training young people to do this work directly. But a more immediate need may be establishing a support group. These programs often serve as vehicles for young men and women in abusive situations to begin to look for help. This section offers details for conducting support groups for teens on family and relationship violence. This guide was developed by Carrie McCluer, not for teaching but for reminding the support group leaders of the skills which they have already learned and which they are now ready to use.

After a general introduction, we list agreements that adult and teen participants in the groups can make with each other, and a rationale ("Some Thoughts About I-Statements") for these agreements. What follows is an in-depth set of instructions, suggestions, and reminders for potential support group leaders, and suggested agenda ideas for a 6–12 session teen support group. The "Protocol for Reporting Child Abuse" details our procedure for California-mandated reporting of child abuse, homicide, suicide, and sexual assault to legal authorities when they are disclosed to us by young people. You will need to consult authorities in your area about appropriate reporting procedures.

WHAT IS A TEEN SUPPORT GROUP?
by Carrie McCluer

A support group is a group of peers meeting together to provide support for each other. BWA calls their groups "Having Healthy Relationships," which includes relationships with family or friends and partners. These groups provide teens with a safe place to talk about themselves and these relationships and to share feelings with other teens, who offer support and feedback. Group members are not identified as victims of abuse but rather as being affected by violence in their life. And the term "violence" covers almost every aspect of a teen's life, either directly or indirectly. A teen has experienced violence just by having grown up in our society, and she/he has something to say about it.

The goal of these groups is to acknowledge and deal with the violence in each group member's life, violence which occurs within all kinds of relationships. While counseling of a sort may occur within these groups, their primary focus is support rather than therapy. The groups begin with general introductions and activities to get to know one another and to increase the sense of safety in the group. Soon the teens are talking about violence and pain and loss, the hard stuff, without prompting from the co-leaders. Because these issues surface so quickly, the teens may feel vulnerable, scared, and unsure about continuing in the group. Co-leaders can help support this process and keep the group together by talking about these feelings.

After acknowledging and talking about this violence, the group moves from looking at individuals and talking about individual problems to group empowerment, creating close and supportive peer relationships that will continue after the group has ended. And by "moves from" I mean it happens on its own. Somehow, a group of teens who really don't know each other, and sometimes don't want to know each other, changes into a group of teens who support each other. And maybe not in ways we would think. Be aware that how they support each other and how we may *want* them to do this are very different.

We talk in this section of the manual about support group co-leaders, but most of the work is really done by the teens looking at themselves and at their relationships with each other. The co-leaders are temporary in this process, a process which continues into the classroom and into new relationships outside the group, even after the group is finished. Closure for the group includes saying good-bye to the group, long-term planning for each member, and possibly referrals to counseling or other types of support systems. Closure may also involve some follow-up with group members, school officials, and parents.

Some of the experiences shared in the group will be reportable; this means they will legally need to be reported to local authorities. This process can be a very difficult one for the teen, the co-leaders, and the other group members. The teen who has disclosed will be concerned about how you will react to the information and how the other teens in the group will react to and use the information. We talk about confidentiality a lot—about keeping what is said within the group. But the reality is that, for teens in a group with their peers from school, confidentiality may be unrealistic. Talking about this fear after a disclosure of abuse is crucial.

Other issues to talk about after abuse has been disclosed include asking the teen what it feels like to tell, asking the others what it's like to hear, and processing any questions about the abuse. We emphasize that sharing the facts isn't necessary, but that the feelings are what we want to hear. This doesn't hold true for everyone. If the teen wants to share the details of the abuse, ask how that is helpful for them, and check it out with the group. This can be hard to hear about, for everyone. But talking about it may be just what everyone needs—somehow the power of the secret is diminished when sharing that secret. Go with the group, and with your gut.

Also, be prepared to support the other group members. They may not be disclosing the abuse, but they are hearing it and having lots of feelings for the one who is disclosing and about their own experiences. As a co-leader hearing the abuse, many of your own issues and your own fears may come up. Reporting can be very scary stuff. Read the section "Protocol for Reporting Child Abuse," and get some support for yourself around this issue.

The entire process of the group will vary according to whether it is a women's, a men's, or a mixed group. There are different strengths and possibilities in each. While we focus here mostly on groups for women victimized by abuse, similar and parallel practices can be used for groups of men dealing with being abused by adults or learning to pass on abuse, or for mixed groups supporting women being powerful and men being allies.

The teens who are members of the support groups held at school, for the most part, have gone through a two-or three-day presentation. After the presentations, teens who are interested in joining a group are asked to sign up (see form, page 142). Other teens may be recommended for this group by faculty at their high school. Those teens who are invited are encouraged to bring their friends and those who they feel would benefit from such a group. This group also provides an opportunity to discuss and explore the feelings that came up for them as they participated in the presentations.

Again, the primary focus of these groups is on teens working with other teens around the issues of violence and abuse. To assist in this process, volunteers are trained to facilitate or "lead" these groups. Volunteers will co-lead each group. "Co-lead" means that two or more people will work together to facilitate the group. It is intended that leaders work together as partners and that no leader is more of a leader than the others. The term "group" also implies that this is not a chance for each member to have a mini-discussion only with the leaders, but that all group members interact with each other. We expect, especially by the end of the group, that group members will be close to each other, that a bond will be established, and that group members will have acknowledged and begun to help each other with personal experiences of abuse.

The ration-ale for running the groups this way is that the program is about empowerment and not therapy, and that we are presenting the group in an edu-cational forum. This program is best at bringing teens to an under-standing of the

Unity Photo: Michael Lichter ©1992

combined power that they can have; we will be leaving them with each other, attempting to bring them to a standpoint from which they can make their own decisions about how to proceed. We can of course help by providing support services and advocacy and, in some places, crisis assistance. But our main function is empowerment. For these same reasons we will aim at conducting the groups less as therapy groups and more as mini-classes; this should push the participants more to help each other. And, not incidentally, by not identifying the group as therapy or the participants as victims, we can avoid, to some extent, having group members stigmatized or identified as victims.

Some Thoughts about I-Statements: Notes on Running a Group
by Allan Creighton

The rules

Early on in the groups we establish some group agreements about talking, maybe even make some group rules about it. These are basically guidelines about communicating well: about speaking for yourself, talking about how you feel, listening effectively to others, and so forth. Great stuff, and important, but sometimes hard to talk about without lapsing into jargon about "shared feelings," "being assertive, not aggressive or passive," and the like. But jargon is not communicative. Not only that, speaking the language of "I-Statements" and "talk about what's going on for you" can sometimes make it sound like all our problems, including violence, would somehow be solved if we just knew how to talk or talk *better* to each other. This misses the point that abused teen women and men, abused children, abused wives, do talk and communicate with the abusers. The problem is not communication.

Maybe a way to get the guidelines going is to notice, in a group, that the rules we have for a group are basically about establishing closeness between people. Setting agreements in the opening group is about getting group members to agree to—commit to—having a relationship with each other, and honoring that relationship. Here are some agreements from our list on pages 9–11, with the reasons for having them.

Rationales for agreements

1. Attendance: you agree to attend all the meetings. This makes sure that everyone is there regularly to contribute, to hear from everyone else, and to be there for her or him.

2. Speaking up: you agree to take a chance, to open up to others, helping others take the same chance to open up to you.

3. Listening: listening—not putting down or trashing or laughing at someone in the group—is about not using these ways to keep yourself apart from other people and not using them to keep you

from feeling the feelings that come up when you are making yourself available to be close.

4. Drugs/Alcohol: you agree not to come to the group stoned or high, so you don't come with a ready-made wall keeping you apart from the others—and apart from yourself.

5. Other agreements: consult our list of agreements for any you wish to add. We highly recommend: I-Statements, No cross-talk, and Having feelings. Ask the group for additional agreements they wish to make.

Really, the guidelines reflect a basic human fact about us: we all have been hurt in various ways, have had lots of experiences of not being listened to well, and so have developed a billion ways to protect ourselves from getting close to each other and becoming vulnerable to further hurt. Sometimes to break these barriers down we have to structure things a bit, use rules. And, of course, we adults sometimes come up with rules to keep ourselves from getting too close to young people or letting them get too close to us. It probably works best to get working consensus among us, adults and teens as a group, to live for the duration of the group by these guidelines and to expect all of us to do so.

Disclosure

This group is not about disclosure of abuse.
   Again:
   This group is not about disclosure of abuse.
   It *is* about dealing with abuse and empowering teens to disclose if it makes sense for them—i.e., helps them, helps free them—to do so. Sometimes we feel that everyone has been abused, everyone has an incident or multiple incidents to talk about, and that we need to get everyone to talk about them because talking will help people "heal." There is an idea just like that in the video *My Girl*: "Talking about it helps the pain to go away."
   The reality is, disclosure hurts. It is painful and embarrassing, and it can *worsen* some situations. The discloser may be left feeling totally humiliated and alone. The rest of us may feel helpless to deal adequately with the abuse disclosed, and all of us are suddenly involved in a painful reporting process. Sometimes there can be a sort of group "ethic" to disclose, and participants will talk about difficult things or events, even against their will, in order to be able to identify with the group. We as group leaders are so eager to be able to reach

and stop abuse that we may help create such a group norm. This inadvertently isolates teens who are too afraid to tell their stories, who feel their own story isn't as dramatic or "awful" as other teens', who don't believe they have stories to tell, or who choose not to tell because they are not ready.

We have to be equal to disclosure—to prepare for its happening, to support teens who disclose, to encourage teens to talk about the deepest and most difficult issues around family and relationship violence and the other kinds of abuses that hit them. We must be strong enough to hear them out and to make it safe for teens to tell. *And,* impossibly, we must make it safe for some teens *not* to tell. Being pushed to disclose will help some victims of abuse get to the point they want to reach. Being allowed to take their time and control the process entirely will give other teens more control over what happens to them than they have ever had.

Probably the best touchstone we have for this difficult balance is to explain this to group members, staying open with them about what we are doing. And to commit ourselves to dealing with and stopping the abuse, whether that involves disclosure or not. We have some help: you can get teens to write anonymously if they don't want to talk. You can get them to talk about how it feels *not* to talk. Or make a rule with them that they won't have to say what they don't want to say, but can work on how it would feel to be able to talk or to have the rest of us committed to being there for them no matter what they say. Sometimes the most important work happens in just this kind of silence. And sometimes nothing happens at all when the victim tells her/his story in detail—the details can bury the feelings. What we go back to, again and again, is supporting the teens making their own decisions and providing information, support, and respect while they do it. And since we are all also on our own paths of recovery, or dealing with abuse, we also need to get help from one another to do this work.

Note that in the "Protocol for Reporting Child Abuse" there is a printed statement on reporting that is suggested for these groups, a statement to be read or presented in some form to let group members know what it means to disclose to us (pages 130–131). Look over the statement and think of how you would like to express it directly, simply, and unthreateningly to a teen group. Try it out with your co-facilitator.

Crying

Part of the group is educative, part of it is practice, part of it is support. Some time during the opening session (along with the other dozen details we have to mention), we can acknowledge that the issues we will bring up affect all of us profoundly and that many feelings will come up—including crying and laughter, and boredom and excitement, and fury, and others. As Vernon says in the video *My Girl*, "It's OK to cry; it's OK to be sensitive."

We want to encourage everyone to take in and to experience the feelings they have. Sometimes, when someone cries we want to fix it, to stop it, to help, or to just make it go away. This is partly because of all the ways we got stopped when we cried around other people. It would be great to get group agreement, then, to recognize that these feelings can be respected and allowed to happen and be supported. Crying can help you clear out feelings, think, alleviate the pain, and bring you out of isolation, pulling a group together. And crying is not easy—it can feel foolish. If you are a man it can be difficult to cry or even to know what feelings you have at all. Establishing group permission for this is terrific. Also, you don't *have* to cry to belong to the group!

And, by the way, one form of crying is yelling. It also can help you clear out. It can also scare everyone away! But a group that can contain anger and not just be "nice" is a powerful group.

THE SUPPORT GROUP LEADER ALLIANCE

A crucial aspect of leading the group is the relationship between the co-leaders. It becomes more crucial in proportion as the leaders differ in age, race, sexual orientation, economic status, etc. Modeling a healthy, respectful relationship across these lines is one of the primary tasks of group leaders. It means checking in with your co-leader, giving the relationship time outside of the group setting, having both of you be part of a support system (at BWA, this is the monthly Support Group Leader meeting). An alliance between African-American and white women, between an older and a younger woman, or between two men of differing ethnicities or sexual orientations plays out exactly the kind of abuse-free relationships we are promoting in the groups—and, incidentally, enables us as leaders to practice what we preach. Among other things, this means looking at these differences and power imbalances as part of our training and as part of our ongoing support systems.

Because the primary issues for these groups are male-to-female and adult-to-young person violence, the Teen Program uses only women leaders for its women's groups, while using men, or a woman and man, to lead teen men's groups. We also encourage young people to assist and to co-lead the groups. Having young people, women, people of color, gay, lesbian, and bisexual people in positions of leadership raises the safety all around and increases the possibilities of stopping the violence exponentially.

The following pages, written by Carrie McCluer, offer some hands-on rules for co-leaders. They can be summarized in a few words: love, honor, and respect for the young people we meet—and for ourselves.

The support group leaders' commitment

▲   to go through training

▲   to meet regularly with other leaders for the sole purpose of supporting one another doing this work

▲   to facilitate setting up the support group

▲   to meet with your co-leader before and after the group

▲   to co-lead the group weekly for approximately 1½ hours

▲   to contact support group members who have stopped attending the group or who have special needs

▲   to acknowledge that as a leader your role is very powerful and helps to set the tone of the group and to establish the communication between group members

▲   to model healthy, mutually respectful relationships with your co-leader

▲   to receive support as a leader from your own family and friends and from other staff and volunteers as needed

▲ SUPPORT GROUP AGREEMENTS

All group members, including teens and adults, make the following agreements for our work together in our meetings, presentations, and support groups. We make the agreements in order to build trust, honor, respect, safety, and closeness among us in the group. (The following are adapted from "Agreements," pages 9–11.)

1. Confidentiality

I agree to keep what comes up in the group confidential and in the group, unless it is dangerous to do so—that is, unless a situation described in the group really requires us to get some outside help. This means that I don't repeat what someone else says in the group outside the group without getting permission from that person. It also means that I don't talk to that person about what they said in the group without getting their permission.

2. Punctuality and attendance

I make a commitment to everyone in the group to be present at all group meetings and to be on time and leave on time. Missing a meeting is grounds for being asked to leave the group.

3. No put-downs

I agree not to put down, make fun of, or trash other people or myself in the group.

4. Right to pass

I understand that I have the right not to talk in the group when I don't want to.

5. Drugs and alcohol

I agree not to participate in the group while under the influence of alcohol or other drugs.

6. Feelings

I recognize that all of us in the group will sometimes experience feelings of hurt, sadness, or anger, and I agree to respect and allow expression of those feelings, including my own.

7. Respect

I agree to listen to others in the group and to expect that the group will listen to me.

Unity Photo: Perry Chow ©1992

8. I-Statements

I agree to speak for myself and my own experiences when talking and not to speak for others unless asked to.

▲   Facilitate *group* communication.
Help the group to talk with each other about what is being said
and about the group dynamics. Steer away from working one-
to-one with a group member while the other members watch.
Keep everyone active in the discussion.

▲   Pull members into the focus of the group.
Notice which group members pull away from the group, either
physically or emotionally. Address this as appropriate.

▲   Be supportive and caring.
Be supportive of the group members and of your co-leaders.
Make time to meet with your co-leaders before the group to
decide on the agenda, and after the group to process what
happened during the group. This also means learning to "read"
your co-leaders, which takes time, and being able to discuss
what feelings come up during the group. This support may
extend to calling the group members and co-leaders during the
week to check in with them.

▲   Listen actively without judging.
This means really listening, rather than preparing what it is you
will say next. And it means listening without placing your own
values on what is said.

▲   Pay attention to power relationships.
Be clear about racial, economic, age, and other differences or
inequalities in the group, and strategize with your co-leaders
about how to acknowledge them.

▲   Work closely with all co-leaders.
In these groups, there is not one leader and one co-leader. There
are two or more co-leaders who work together, deciding on the
agenda of the group and providing support for all of the group
members.

▲   Act as a counselor/teacher/friend without counseling, teaching,
or giving advice!

▲   Ensure the physical safety of the group members.

▲   Ensure the emotional safety of the group members.

Remember to

▲   Listen actively without interrupting or judging.

▲   Accept the person's feelings.
Because feelings are feelings, they are never "right" or "wrong."
They just are, and they deserve acceptance and respect.

▲   Support the person doing for her/himself.
Rather than taking control and taking on the burden of doing for
the person, leave the responsibility for action on the group
member. Help the group member build her or his own solutions
by asking what he or she wants to do and wants to have happen.
Prioritizing these wants and looking at first steps is helpful. It
may also be helpful to ask how the group members can be
supportive of the person doing this.

▲   Respond to what is being said with appropriate feeling words
and with nonjudgmental phrasing.
Possible statement beginnings to use include "How do you feel
about—", "Tell me more about—". Summarize what was said to
help clarify.

▲   Name the feelings that go along with what is being said.
All kinds of information may be given without being associated
with any feelings about what happened. Reflect back what was
said with a feeling word attached: "You seem to be feeling—"
or, "What I hear you say is that you felt—" may be appropriate
sentence beginnings.

▲   Use the power of silence.
Sometimes it is hard to just be silent in a group. Rather than
filling up the space with your words, it may be best to wait.
Keep in mind that silence is the opportunity to think and get in
touch with feelings.

▲   Be aware of your body language, voice quality, and vocabulary.
Your body and voice can be used to convey messages and
feelings. What messages are you giving, both consciously and
unconsciously? Listen to the words you use. Are they appropriate for this group?

▲   Be aware of the welfare of the group.
Ask yourself, "Is what is happening benefiting the *whole* group?"

▲   Be responsive to the needs of the group.
The agenda is used to facilitate the group process. If what has

been planned for the day seems inappropriate, be prepared with an alternate agenda or activity, or ask the group what they would like to do and go with that instead.

▲ Help group members deal with abuse.
Keep in mind that the support group is not about disclosure, but about supporting group members. For some group members this may mean disclosing the details of abuse; for others talking about the feelings associated with the abuse is what is needed. Check it out with the person disclosing; she or he. They will be able to tell you what she/he needs from the group.

▲ Respect confidentiality.
It is important to respect the confidentiality of what happens in the group, while also remembering the reporting laws.

▲ Make referrals as needed.
It may be appropriate to refer a group member to another agency or to one-to-one counseling to get more support.

and ask yourself "What is going on for me?" if you find yourself

▲ Giving advice or doing therapy

▲ Having strong reactions to someone who is of a different age, gender, race, or sexual orientation from you, or if you notice that these people never seem to have anything to say

▲ Telling someone what to do

▲ Giving "should messages," or becoming judgmental or critical

▲ Rescuing or "doing for" someone

▲ Getting angry at or giving up on someone because they seem stuck or are unable or unwilling to act on their own behalf

▲ Attempting to provide support you are not qualified to give

▲ Offering material assistance

▲ Establishing "personal" relationships or giving out your home phone number

▲ Making promises you are unable to keep

▲ Feeling inadequate or overwhelmed

Proceed with

▲ Maintain clear boundaries.
Remember, support group leaders provide support. This support is very important, and also very limited. After the group, the group members return to their homes and their lifestyles. It is not the role of the support group leader to "save" someone or to become that person's only support system. The role does include helping the group member to better handle their situation and to make appropriate lifestyle choices.

▲ Be aware of your own issues.
Your own issues and feelings will come up. Be aware of them and make time to discuss them with someone else later.

▲ Notice when you are problem-solving rather than listening.
Sometimes it is easier as listeners to see clear solutions to another's problems. However, if you move into problem-solving before the talker is ready to do so, the talker will not feel listened to and will feel pushed to do what is suggested.

▲ Notice when you are lecturing or giving advice.
When lecturing, your own value systems take over, without considering the values of the person with whom you are talking. When giving information, provide the information that is asked for, but watch out for giving advice instead. Giving information is not the same as solving a person's problem for her or him.

▲ Watch out for "Why?" questions.
"Why" is a very loaded word and can be attached to feelings of self-blame and guilt. Try to use "How is it—", "What do you think about—", "Tell me more about—" or another phrase instead.

▲ Think about self-disclosure.
Remember, whoever is doing the talking is getting the support. This does not mean that it is never OK to self-disclose. It does

mean that it is important to think about how and what it is you want to disclose, and what you hope to have happen because you have disclosed. Keep in mind the importance of putting the needs of the group before your own needs. Group leaders are group members, but to a different degree. This is a hard issue, and there are no "rules" about disclosing. Decide how you feel about disclosing, and decide what you are willing to disclose. Just keep in mind that whoever does the talking gets the help.

Some things co-leaders need from each other

▲ To be there—this means emotionally for me, as well as physically attending each group.

▲ To be a *co*-leader, rather than a leader. To be willing to work with me and to work together.

▲ To be committed to doing the group, and to being on time. To keep any commitments you make.

▲ To communicate your needs to me and to accept me non-judgmentally.

▲ To take a more active role in the group when I need to pull away or when I miss something. To take responsibility for the group and step in when necessary.

▲ To build good communication skills—with the group members and with me, too.

▲ To be open and direct. To be able to discuss conflicts between us. To be a friend to me and give me time to talk about my issues outside of the group.

▲ Feedback—I want to know how you see the progress of the group and to know how you see the way I work with the group.

▲ To be open to my ideas and flexible with the agenda.

▲ To be creative, to take risks, and to take chances with yourself as well as with the group. To have the strength to confront.

▲ To be committed to self-liberation and to support others in becoming liberated as well. To be an ally for me and to address the "isms."

▲ To have faith in the potential for growth in all of the group members.

▲　　To have a sense of humor and an ability to play.

Group safety

Part of our role as support group leaders is to ensure the safety of the group members. Some of the ways we have come up with to help the group members feel safe are to

▲　Maintain the group agreements

▲　Facilitate group interaction

▲　Help everyone fit into the group

▲　Be friendly and welcoming to group members and make eye contact

▲　Introduce new group members to each other

▲　Convey that all group members are valued and that it is important that they have joined the group

▲　Acknowledge feelings and give support

▲　Avoid putting anyone on the spot too soon

▲　Ensure that everyone participates

▲　Keep the group interesting and entertaining

▲　Provide nourishment—meet the needs of the group members

▲　Unconditionally respect all of the group members

▲　Be organized and respectful of everyone's time

▲　Throw out the agenda when appropriate

▲　Participate as a group member while being mindful of the needs of the group

▲　Do check-ins or an exercise to open the group and an activity to close the group

▲　Meet in a circle with no extra chairs in a comfortable room

SETTING UP A SUPPORT GROUP

We do many different kinds of support groups. Some at high schools after school, some at the high schools during class time at the request of a teacher, some at a Girls' Center or Juvenile Hall, and some onsite at our offices. Most of the information in this manual pertains to any kind of group, but the information below about setting up a support group is designed for use with an after-school group at a high school.

1. Meet with the liaison at the school to decide what day and time will best meet the needs of the school and the students.

2. Pick a room which is the most comfortable for the group. Look for a room with chairs rather than desks, with carpeting if possible, and in a location familiar to the students.

3. Get sign-ups from interested students who have seen the classroom presentations in their class. (See form, page 137.)

4. Talk with teachers, counselors, vice principals, etc., to get referrals of possible support group members.

5. Meet with all co-leaders and discuss agenda ideas and any concerns.

6. Revise or create an invitation to send out to the students at school. (See form, page 138.)

7. Two weeks before the group begins, confirm date, time, and room with the liaison.

8. One week before the group begins, send the invitations to the students. Ask the liaison to give them to the students during class.

9. A few days before the group begins, contact the potential group members by phone and remind them of the group.

10. Meet with the co-leaders and discuss any last minute concerns, questions, etc. Be sure you have enough parent permission slips to hand out on the first day. (See form, page 139.)

After the group has begun, two forms are used by the co-leaders to aid in keeping track of statistics. One form (page 140) outlines the planned agenda and compares this to "what actually happened." The second (page 143) is the Teen Information Form, which is completed for each teen we have individual or group contact with. This form is updated weekly so we know who attended which group and what took place in the interaction.

SUPPORT GROUP AGENDA IDEAS

Usually, each group begins with a brief review of the group agreements. A check-in follows. Check-ins can be general or may begin with a specific question to set the topic for the meeting. Sometimes a check-in is enough, and the group will continue on its own. At other times, one or more opening activities is appropriate. A short group exercise can also be used to set the tone. A more in-depth exercise can follow, as well as some type of discussion. The groups should be concluded in such a way as to provide closure. This may mean ending with a brief summary of what happened, asking the group members how they feel now that the session is ending, or doing appreciations.

It is most important for you to remember that you already have the information and know the activities you need to facilitate these groups. The sample agendas below are just to give you some ideas and options, especially if a particular subject is brought up by the group members. Usually, by the end of the first group the members have talked enough about themselves for you to know what issues are appropriate for that group. Try the ideas we have listed—keep what works and throw out what doesn't work. And if the co-leaders' agenda about that subject isn't working, *toss it*! Also, keep in mind that these exercises may not be appropriate for all groups.

Unity Photo: Nic Paget-Clarke ©1992

Feel free to ask the group what they want to do. One of the goals is to have group members really run the group. Yes, we may begin the group and act as "traffic lights," helping the process of the group, but the members themselves will make the group a real success. And the only way you will know what they need, and they will get what they need is if you ask them. So, go ahead and ask—and ask in such a way that they will tell you.

The following are sample agendas for 12 group meetings.

Week One: Introductions

▲ Co-leaders introduce themselves

▲ Discuss the purpose and goals of the group

▲ Review the support group agreements

▲ Hand out permission slips

▲   Group members introduce themselves, state their names and why they are here

▲   Possible Group Exercises:
— Icebreaker/Inclusion Activity (see page 126)
— Comfort circle (see page 128)

Week Two: Growing up male/female

▲   Check-in

▲   Party roleplay

▲   Men Stand-Up/Women Stand-Up

▲   Discuss myths and messages about what women/men are supposed to be. Discuss feelings about these messages
— What one thing do we never want to hear again?
— Personal experiences of being hurt because of our gender
— What do we like about being male/female?

Week Three: Sexuality and relationships

▲   Check-in

▲   Define "What is a relationship?"

▲   Exercise: Write down three beliefs about sex on one side of a sheet of paper and three fears about sex on the other. Put these in a hat, pass them around, pick one, and read it aloud as if it were your own

▲   Party roleplay
— Discuss male/female roles
— What is expected of us?

▲   Agree to watch a couple in real-life to discuss at the next meeting

Week Four: Violence against women and young people

▲   Check-in

▲   Discuss observations of couples (see "homework" from last group)

▲   What would you say to that couple, to the person in power, or to others in similar situations?

▲   Re-enact one of the situations observed. Now re-do it and take charge of the situation

Week Five: Racism

▲ Check-in, including naming a hero or heroine of your own ethnicity and what it is you admire about them

▲ Define racism and the terms "people of color"/"white"

▲ Discussion: Brainstorm and list
  — What are examples of racism that have happened to each different group of color? (List each separately)
  — What are ways that young white people have gotten the message that people of color are "less than" whites?
  — Where do these lies come from? Why are they passed on?
  — Define internalized oppression

▲ Activity (if it is safe in the group)
  — Ask one person of color to talk about ways they have been hurt by racism
  — Ask one white person to talk about any early experience of learning that people of color were less than or different from whites, and how that affected them
  — Same-race dyads, then process in a group

▲ Discussion
  — Explain why we believe there is no such thing as reverse racism
  — How would you like things to be?
  — What can you do to help stop racism?

Week Six: Heterosexism

▲ Check-in, including naming someone of your own gender whom you are close to, and what you like/love about your relationship

▲ Discussion: Brainstorm and list
  — Define gay/lesbian/bisexual/heterosexual
  — What were the *first* messages you received about gays/lesbians/bisexuals?
  — What names do gays/lesbians/bisexuals get called?
  — What stereotypes have you heard?

▲ Discussion
  — These names are hurtful; the stereotypes are untrue. Where do you think this "information" comes from?
  — Why?

▲ Define homophobia and heterosexism

▲ Visualization
— Lead the group, consciously thinking of themselves as "heterosexuals," through a Friday at school and then out on a date, then talking about the date with family and friends in a society where heterosexuals are seen as "not-the-norm"
— Dyad: How does this feel?

▲ (Alternative Activity) Dyads
— Talk with your dyad partner about a current or past relationship without using a he/she pronoun, doing your best not to identify the gender of the other person. Group process on what it's like to have to hide or to "pass"

▲ Activity: Dyads
— Lie in the arms of someone of the same gender, and process how it feels, three minutes each way

▲ Discussion
— In a heterosexual society, how are gays/lesbians/bisexuals oppressed?
— How does homophobia affect us?
— Think of any ways you act or alter your behavior or speech in order not to be seen as gay, lesbian, or bisexual
— How does heterosexism affect us?
— How have you or people you know been hurt?
— What steps can you take to stop homophobia/heterosexism?

Week Seven: Adultism

▲ Check-in

▲ Teen Visualization (see page 99)

▲ Adultism Visualization and Teens Stand-Up

▲ Group process

Week Eight: Personal experience of violence

▲ Check-in

▲ Exercise: 10 minutes of silent writing. Write about a personal experience of violence.

▲ Discuss the feelings, not necessarily the details

▲ It may be appropriate to create a continuum of violence if the different experiences of group members vary in severity. In this way, everyone can see that they are not alone in their experiences, that all violence hurts, and that violence hurts us all, no matter what its duration or intensity.

Week Nine: Power—getting help

▲ Check-in

▲ Exercise: Power Shuffle

▲ Discuss and define "power"

▲ Power chart

▲ Nonpower visualization

Week Ten: Relationships among women/men

▲ Check-in

▲ Icebreaker

▲ Discussion
  — What is safe/not safe to share with the same gender?
  — What are the risks?
  — How can we secure safe relationships?
  — What are realistic expectations of close friends?
  — Relationships across cultural lines/outside family

▲ Exercise: A pair of friends within the group discusses their relationship. What's good? Hard? Next?

Week Eleven: Family

▲ Check-in

▲ Spend 10 minutes drawing a picture of your family silently— you decide who your family is

▲ Spend 10 minutes writing about what you learned as part of your family, what your family means to you, something you learned about relationships from being in your family, how you feel about being a member of your family

▲ Share what you would like us to know about your family. You can share your drawing, your writing, or both—as you wish.

Week Twelve: Closure/life plans/appreciations/goodbyes

▲ Check-in: how are you feeling about ending this group?

▲ Discuss long-term plans. What's next?

▲ Possible Group Exercises/Appreciations
— Re-do Comfort Circles—have they changed? (see page 128)
— Write appreciations on a card
— Write appreciations on a piece of paper attached to the back of each group member
— Whisper appreciations to group members standing in the middle of the room with eyes closed

Other group agenda ideas

Check-ins/icebreakers/inclusion activities

▲ Introduce yourself with your name and a same first-letter word which describes you.

▲ Tell us about your name. Who gave it to you? How did they decide on that name? Do you like your name? What is your nickname?

▲ Stand in a circle and show how you feel today without using words.

▲ Draw a picture of how you are feeling today. Others either shout out their guesses like a game, or the person draws and spends time sharing.

▲ If you could spend the evening visiting with any person dead or alive, who would it be? Why?

▲ If your life were a song, movie, or book title, what would it be? Why?

▲ What have you had to learn to grow up in your family?

▲ What is one thing somebody in this group does not know about you?

▲ On slips of paper, each person in the group silently writes an adjective to describe what they thought of each group member the very first time they met them. The facilitators give these out anonymously. Then each person looks at them and shares their favorite one with the group.

▲ On a 5x8 card, write three words ending with "—ing" or "—able" to describe yourself. On the other side, write three facts about yourself. Decide which side to share.

▲ Write your name vertically on paper. Add words to describe yourself which begin with each letter of your name.

▲ Chain Question: each group member takes a turn asking one person in the group a personal question. That person then asks someone else a question, until everyone has been asked one question.

▲ Bring one thing from home which represents you.

▲ The Differences exercise: people get into dyads with themes such as: "Find someone with a different birth month than you have." After they have found a partner (if necessary, make one group of three), give them something to discuss for two minutes, such as "How do you like to spend your birthday?"

▲ A good check-in opening is a question that ties in with the agenda topic for that day. Some ideas:
— Someone who has taught me something important
— What kind of animal/tree/color/season do I feel like today
— If I were a flavor of ice-cream I would be _____
— How I select my friends
— What I value most in a friend is _____
— Something good in my life right now is _____
— Three things my family says about me, my teachers/friends say about me, I say about myself, or I think support group members say about me
— What I like most/least about being male/female
— Someone from my own ethnic group I look up to and why

▲ Or, you can ask each member to finish a sentence opener. Some ideas:
— I feel _____
— I want _____
— I have to _____
— I wish I was _____
For other ideas consult any book on "new games" for young people.

Group exercises

▲ Any kind of drawing or artwork.

▲ Sharing a Secret: each group member writes a secret they have never told anyone about themselves on a piece of paper. Mix up the papers. Each group member takes a turn reading one of the secrets as if it were his or her own and talks about what it is like to have that secret. Other group members give feedback about the secret, about their own experiences of that secret, and about how they feel about people who have that secret. Many times, more than one person has the same secret. After discussion, the owner of the secret chooses to own their secret or not.

▲ "If You Really Knew Me, You'd Know": each group member is given three minutes to talk, beginning each sentence with, "If you really knew me, you'd know . . . . " If they run out of things to say, they are to repeat the same things over and over. Then the group has two minutes to ask questions before moving on to the next group member. Three minutes may be hard, but stick to it! Wonderful things are said when given the time!

▲ As a group, spend 10 minutes writing and 10 minutes drawing how you feel today. Then share with the others. This activity is appropriate for drawing/writing about anything!

▲ Drawing a Comfort Circle: A comfort circle is a drawing which depicts how much each person shares with others or chooses to keep private. The drawing is of three concentric circles. The innermost circle represents information about yourself which you share with no one. The middle circle is how much you share with close friends. And the outermost circle is how much you share with the general public. Everyone has a different Comfort Circle, with each concentric circle being a different size. Some people may choose to create a very different type of drawing.

Each person, taking turns, draws their Comfort Circle and explains what it means to them. The other group members then have a chance to ask questions. This is a fun exercise to use when talking about what is safe to share with others and, specifically, what is safe to share with the group.

▲ Draw a timeline of your life, or do a life map with pictures. Include your past, present, and future. Option—create this with photos cut out of magazines glued to paper. Discuss how these events in your life have affected you. Is there a theme to your life? How would you describe someone who has had these life events?

▲ Draw on one side of the paper how you think others see you. Draw on the other side how you really are. Option—cut out photos to depict how others see you and glue to the outside of a paper bag, and place items inside which really represent you. Spend time talking about what it's like to have people judge each other by what they see on the outside, never knowing what is inside.

There are an infinite number of possibilities. Try out anything you think might work. And when it does, add it to this list.

PROTOCOL FOR REPORTING CHILD ABUSE
by Allan Creighton

Note: *This section describes BWA/California procedures on reporting. You must consult authorities in your region to determine appropriate procedures for your area.*

The law

BWA staff and volunteers are mandated reporters of child abuse. Stated or suspected physical and/or sexual abuse of any person under age 18 must be reported, and mental abuse may be reported. Reports must be made when the mandated reporter (quoting from the law)

> "has knowledge of or observes a child in his or her professional capacity or within the scope of his or her employment, whom he or she knows or reasonably suspects has been the victim of child abuse. For the purpose of this article, 'reasonable suspicion' means that it is objectively reasonable for a person to entertain such a suspicion, based upon facts that could cause a reasonable person in a like position, drawing when appropriate on his or her training and experience, to suspect child abuse." (California Penal Code 11166)

Designated reporters

In institutional settings where we provide workshops and support groups for teens, BWA will secure an institutional staff-person to be the designated reporter of abuse. This does not lessen our responsibility, but it does involve the institution in immediate and follow-up advocacy and support for teens who disclose abuse. In all cases where abuse is disclosed, BWA Teen Program personnel must inform onsite staff and must follow up with the institution's designated reporter to make certain that the report has been issued. Sometimes this system does not work—the designated reporter may be remiss or may not be available—and we have to file reports regardless.

Teachers and reporting

Teachers are mandated reporters, and so are we, as presenters in the classroom and support group leaders. However, as "visitors" we have very different issues to deal with regarding reporting than teachers, who may feel protective of their classes. A teacher may feel like a confidant of a student. She/he is a daily contact for the teen. Teachers have differing attitudes about abuse, ranging from collusion or minimization, to guilt or fear about reporting, to their own full strategy for working with an abused teen. We like to have teachers fully informed about the reporting process—their responsibilities and ours—before we go into the class. However, the reality is we cannot expect them to be fully aware, and we often find that they do not know the law.

Regardless of a teacher's position on reporting, if you *know of* or *suspect* child abuse, you must report it. The designated reporter will usually not be the teacher, so you need not notify the teacher that you are making a report. However, it is safe to assume that the teacher will learn that a report has been made on one of their students and that you were involved in this process. Some teachers will be supportive of your actions. Others will feel that you have jeopardized their trust with this student and possibly with the entire class.

Alerting teens

We want to create an environment safe for students to disclose abuse if they so choose, and we want to work with them to obtain resources to stop or prevent abuse. For some teens, this may be the first time they have mentioned the experience at all, or realized that they have been abused. We want to encourage teens to talk in any way they feel most comfortable and to enable and empower them to decide where and how to disclose. As part of this process we must give notice of the reporting law in our opening encounters with the teens, in any classroom or support group setting where we expect disclosures to happen. The notice can be a formal statement like that on page 129, or a simpler, more direct statement may be:

> What we talk about in this room is confidential with three exceptions: one, if I think you are going to hurt yourself; two, if I think you are going to hurt someone else; and three, if I think someone or something is hurting you or has hurt you in the past, including your parent(s). When any of these things is going on, I will need to let someone know and try to get additional help for you.

Note that we use the word "refer" in place of "report"; this is an attempt to reframe the context of reporting. The reporting process is not about turning teens in, but rather about getting them help. Of course, no matter how we frame it, the process, once initiated, will sometimes feel to them and to us like a betrayal of confidence. It is crucial for us to be clear that this process is about *getting help*.

Anonymous writings

Generally, we get anonymous writings from teens about their personal experiences of violence. The writings give us information, enable them to identify with the issues, and, for some of them, constitute a first attempt at disclosing abuse. We tell the teens that these writings are anonymous, and we must make a concerted effort to keep them so. This means

1. Telling students that these writings are anonymous.

2. Telling students that if they *wish* to put their names on these writings they may, and we will contact them after class or at some other time. We will not contact them at home unless they write in a home phone number and ask us to call them.

3. Collecting the writings in such a way as not to put faces with stories—having students leave them face down on a table, and not reading them until after class.

4. Not letting teachers read these writings, because they can connect handwriting with faces. This means we never ask teachers to identify someone by their handwriting.

There will be unusual instances—a teen hands you a writing directly, face up, in tears—instances that *may* be cries for help. You need to trust your instincts. Sometimes the situation will be manipulated by a teen so that their cry for help is heard without them directly telling you. This can be tricky, leaving a presenter very confused about what to do. If this happens, talk to a co-presenter or another program staff member for support, information, and suggestions. The bottom line is that, if all precautions are made to keep writings anonymous and you still *know* or *suspect* that abuse is happening with an identified student, a report must be made.

The process

So, here is the teen, standing in front of you, who has just told you she or he is being abused. What next? Let's start with the situation in which the teen is unequivocally asking for help. In the following scenario we will presume the teen is a young woman, but the process applies, of course, to young men as well. (In the following, "CPS" refers to Child Protective Services, the agency mandated reporters notify in California. Substitute the appropriate reporting agency for your region.)

1. The *first* thing to do is to remember that you are an advocate for her, backing her up to take as much power and control over the situation as is legally allowed.

2. Find a place where you can talk for a few moments. This may happen in the empty classroom or the room next door. The teacher may or may not be part of it, depending on what the teen wants and your sense of the teacher's capacity to help. Her best friend may be part of it, depending on what she wants. This may be the point when you involve the designated reporter, who will be part of the process from here on.

3. Assess the danger of the situation and what the teen's next 24 hours are going to be like. Is the abuser currently a threat? Where is the abuser? Does the teen have immediate alternatives for getting away?

4. Explain the reporting process and what CPS does. Encourage her to make the call herself, with you and the teacher (if applicable) as support.

5. If she can't make the call, try to make sure that you or the teacher or her best friend, etc., can be with her while you or the designated reporter calls.

6. Alert the designated reporter if he or she has not been involved so far. If the designated reporter is included from the outset, they will probably do the report. Otherwise, you may be doing the report with support from the designated reporter.

7. Make the call. If the abuse told to you is being done or has been done by a family member or nonfamily member within the home, call CPS. If it is being done or has been done by someone outside the home (this includes dating violence), call the police. If in doubt, simply call CPS. When calling CPS ask to speak to a caseworker.

8. CPS (or the police) will, in the majority of cases, simply take the information. They may refer the teen to counseling or make an appointment for the teen to come in. This age group is lowest in

their priorities, and they are overworked. You will need to be prepared to support the teen when this happens. It may feel like a letdown, or a relief; it may seem to the teen like no one is taking her seriously. As an advocate, you are still with her, figuring out with her what the next step is.

CPS may decide to come out. In this case, try to stay, or arrange for someone else to stay with the teen until they come. It is nerve-wracking for her, and she may want to run away, or deny, or hide. This is the time to go over her life-plan with her: how to handle the next 24 hours, who her best friends and support persons are, where a safe place to stay might be, and how she feels about all this.

9. Part of this final planning will be working out with the teen if she wants to stay in touch with you. You can give her the crisis and office phone numbers, and get a safe phone number from her if it is available. We discourage you from giving your home phone number: the abuser could get your number. Also, because this is a time of crisis for the teen, she may be ready to get you more involved in the crisis than you want to be.

What if the teen won't participate, starts denying what happened, or disappears? Basically, you follow the above process without the teen. If the teen disappears, you may want to strategize with the teacher, best friend, or designated reporter about the teen's safety and about how to reconnect with the teen. The reporting process can seem very intimidating, and denial and disappearance are obvious coping mechanisms. You need to report and to trust your judgment about reconnecting with the teen.

Where/when to report

Reportable abuse must be reported to Children's Protective Services or the police by phone immediately.

Written reports

A written report must follow within 36 hours. The agency you notify should have the appropriate form, and will work with you to fill it out.

Following up/letting go

Based on what you plan with the teen, you may be in for some days or weeks of contact with her. You can choose to take this on, or you can refer it to an appropriate local agency. If the teen is removed from the home, however, the CPS worker and foster-home personnel may stop this contact. The teen herself may feel betrayed and may break off contact. You need to be able to accept this, and let go. You have done what you could and have to trust that she is on her way out of an abusive situation in the best way she can manage. She gets to decide whether to continue with you, and you get to be an advocate—not a friend, or a social relationship, or a protector, or savior. This may be hard for you. You should get total support from your program staff for getting through it. Total support.

Reporting is not pleasant for anyone. The child or teen will need your support and at the same time may be angry at you for telling. She/he will need long-term advocacy, and you will need support from your co-workers and staff. Get the support. You must remember that, however hard reporting is, the long-term consequences are crucial for the survival of the young person. Even with the worst outcome to this process—say, that CPS minimizes what happens, the teen is back in the home, and the situation is still dangerous—the teen has asked for help, has been heard, and knows that the abuse does not have to happen and can be fought. They will get through it, and will have escaped an abusive situation with your help. This work is liberation.

To Conclude

As a teacher, role model, and ally for young people, your work helps stop the violence that destroys our youth. From this book you should now have new understandings and activities for making your work more effective. Talk with other adults about the material in this book. Share it with the young people you live or work with.

You can't do it all at once. Pick some activities to try out that you can incorporate into what you are already doing. Start slowly, and build support and enthusiasm from those around you. Expand on the material presented here. Modify it, adapt it, be creative. And let us know what you come up with.

BWA and OMP are available for trainings and technical assistance. Good luck and keep in touch.

Appendix

Unity Photo: Doug Brugge ©1992

This is a gathering of forms we have used in conducting our programs. It includes pre- and posttests, surveys, sign-up sheets, and the like, as well as a variety of evaluation forms so teens and teachers can respond to us about what we do.

Please keep in mind that all of these are *samples* from the BWA Teen Program and must be adapted to meet your needs.

A Personal Experience of Violence

Please write a paragraph on each of the following questions. You can write as freely as you like. You do not have to write your name on this paper if you feel more comfortable staying anonymous. But if you would like a follow-up contact from the Teen Program, please include your name. You can write on both sides of this paper.

1. Describe an experience in which you were hurt or made to feel unsafe by someone at school, in your neighborhood, or family. What happened, how did it make you feel, and what did you do about it?

2. If this is happening to you now, what can you do about it?

If you are in trouble now, or someone you know is in trouble, you can get help. You can call Battered Women's Alternatives at Contra Costa County Crisis and Suicide Prevention, at 930-8300. You can call anytime and you don't have to give your name if you don't want to. You can also call if you have any questions about what we are talking to you about or about what services we provide.

_____ High School

Date _____

BWA's Teen Program will soon be offering an after-school Women's Group at your high school. This group will focus on talking with each other about growing up female and male, dating, and having healthy relationships and friendships with men and other women.
Are you interested? If so, SIGN UP HERE! We'll contact you.

Name	**Phone Number**	**Grade**

Thanks! We'll be in touch soon!

BWA, P.O. Box 6406, Concord CA 94524

_____ **High School**

Date _____

Hello!

You are invited to BWA Teen Program's Women's Group to talk with other women from your school about growing up female, dating, and having healthy relationships and friendships with men and other women. This group will meet every week. It's happening at

Place: _____

Date: _____

Time: _____

Please come! It's going to be fun, it's going to be powerful, and you'll make some new, strong friends. What a great way to spend an afternoon. See YOU there!

Signed,

BWA, P.O. Box 6406, Concord CA 94524

Battered Women's Alternatives and

_____ **High School**

To: Parents of _____
From: Battered Women's Alternatives Teen Program
RE: Teen Women's After-School Group

We would like your permission to allow your daughter _____
_____ to participate in our after-school women's group on building healthy, violence-free relationships. The group will discuss issues pertain-
ing to having healthy relationships with friends and family and in dating
relationships. The group meets weekly for approximately eight weeks, on
_____, at _____ High School. Your daughter
will be in a group of from 8–10 young women from the school, facilitated by
group counselor-educators from BWA. The BWA counselor-educators will be
accountable to BWA staff. If, at any time, you have any questions regarding
your daughter's progress, please feel free to call _____ during
business hours at the Teen Program's office, _____-_____.

- -

I hereby give permission for _____ to attend BWA's
after-school teen women's group at _____ High School. I also
give permission for the BWA counselor-educators to discuss pertinent information with school personnel when it is in the best interest of my daughter.

_____   _____
Signature of Parent/Guardian   Date

This consent for group attendance is valid through this school year, unless
otherwise indicated.

Teen Program Women's Support Group

Date of Group: _____   Session #: _____

Participants: Facilitators:

Planned Agenda   **Topic:**

Check-in:

Activity/Discussion Topic(s):

Closing:

What Actually Happened?

Ideas for Future Sessions:

Using the Teen Information Form

Note: These procedures were developed specifically for volunteers and staff in the BWA Teen Program and should be adapted for use by your group.

What is it?

The Teen Information Form was designed for two purposes. First, it is an easy way for us to remember the particulars of the teens we work with, i.e., age, city, and contact. Second, the form helps us to keep track of the number of teens we work with each month. These numbers may be used in the future for grant-writing, etc., to ensure we are able to continue providing services to teens.

When do I use it?

Each time you meet individually with a teen, or talk with a teen after a presentation, or meet with a teen in a group, or talk with a teen on the phone, fill out a form. If this is a teen you have met or talked with before, just update the form already begun for them.

How do I use it?

After you have spoken with the teen, write in or circle the information the teen gives you on the left-hand side of the form. Write a summary of the contact you had with the teen on the right-hand side of the form. Include the outcome of the contact, the referrals the teen was given, and what steps are next for the teen to make.

Note that you probably will not have some or most of the information on the left side. Just indicate what you do know about the teen—it may be inappropriate for you to have some of this information! Ask only for that which the teen can give you. Safety is a big issue for anyone wanting to share their thoughts and feelings with another. Part of being safe is sharing only what feels safe to share.

If a teen approaches you after a classroom presentation, let's say, and you only know the person's gender and ethnicity and how it is you were contacted by them, just give that information. These sheets are primarily to assist us, not to make more work, and not to pry into areas the teen does not share with us voluntarily.

What do I do with it after I've filled it out?

Return it to your program staff. Take blank forms with you when you will be meeting with teens. After you have completed the form, either mail it in, drop it by, or keep it until the next time you meet.

Abbreviations used

Ethnicity:
L = Latino/a
B = Black/African-American
W = White
A = Asian/Pacific Islander
NA = Native American

Relationship status:
S = single
M = married
LT = long-term but not married

Teen Information

Write in or circle the information given to you. It may not be appropriate for you to have some of this information. Please DO NOT ask for what the teen may be unable to share.

First name _____

Last name _____

City _____

High School _____

Phone _____ Age _____

Is it safe for us to call?   Y   N
Who should we say is calling?
_____

Ethnicity: L   B   W   A   NA   Other _____
Contact: Phone call   Class presentation
Support group   Teen advocacy
Relationship status: S   M   LT   Dating
Length of relationship: _____
children: _____ Ages: _____

Pregnant?	Y	N
Living at home?	Y	N
Threatening suicide?	Y	N
Violence in family?	Y	N
Violence in relationship?	Y	N
Caller is: abused abuser		
Suspect child abuse?	Y	N
CPS involved?	Y	N
Police involved?	Y	N

Someone else who knows? _____

Teacher _____ Phone: _____

CPS worker _____ Phone: _____

Counselor _____ Phone: _____

Other _____ Phone: _____

Use alcohol?   Y   N
Use other drugs?   Y   N
   marijuana   crack   cocaine
   heroin   prescription   other:
Have weapons? Y   N   What?
Working? Y   N   Has car?   Y   N

Topics Discussed

General information   Suicide
Alcohol/other drugs   Counseling
Family issues   Support Group
Relationship issues   Housing
Pregnancy/birth control
Other _____

Summary

Is follow-up needed?
_____

By whom?
_____

Is this relationship ongoing? Y   N
Is teen in danger now?   Y   N
Life-plan for next 48 hours? _____

Write a brief summary of the contact you had with the teen. Include a description of the topics and options discussed. What was the outcome? Write down referrals given, and what step(s) is(are) next

Date of contact   **Volunteer name**

Teen Program Pretest

Age_____ Grade_____ Female/Male   Date_____

	Agree	Disagree
1. Violence happens in very few teenage dating relationships	___	___
2. It's natural for boys to be aggressive and hit others when they are angry	___	___
3. Women who stay in abusive relationships have no one but themselves to blame for their problems	___	___
4. Men who beat women are mentally ill	___	___
5. Some girls like to be hit	___	___
6. Men should make the big decisions in a marriage	___	___
7. Drinking and using drugs affects one's ability to control anger	___	___
8. It is rape when a husband forces his wife to have sex with him	___	___
9. Men are the victims of sexual assault almost as often as women	___	___
10. Teen relationships are often destroyed because of drugs and alcohol	___	___
11. Children deserve to be beaten if they are causing problems at home	___	___
12. There are very few alternatives for men and women who are victims of abuse	___	___

THIS SPACE FOR YOUR ADDRESS

Teen Program Posttest

Age_____   Grade_____   Female/Male   Date_____

1. Describe a time when you have been a victim of violence or acted violently. What did you do about it then, and what would you do about it now?

2. What are some of the reasons that abuse occurs in teenage relationships?

3. Why do some women and men stay in abusive relationships?

4. What are boys taught that might lead them to violence when they grow up?

5. What is rape?

6. How will you stop yourself from hitting the next time you are angry at someone?

7. How can a man and a woman work together to make decisions in a relationship?

(continued)

(Teen Program Posttest, continued)

8. How can you help someone who has been hurt by abuse?

9. How can you help someone who is hurting someone?

10. Why don't many guys who have been sexually abused report it?

11. How could your friendships with people of different racial backgrounds be made stronger?

12. Is it rape when a husband forces his wife to have sex with him? Why or why not?

13. How do drinking or abusing other drugs affect your ability to control your anger?

14. How could it affect you if someone in your family drank or used drugs too much?

15. If you could change anything about your family and friendships right now, what would it be?

Teen Program
Posttest on Family/Teen Violence
and Program Evaluation

Age_____   Grade_____   Male/Female   Date_____

		Agree	Disagree
1.	Serious violence happens in relatively few marriages and relationships	_____	_____
2.	Men who beat women are mentally ill	_____	_____
3.	Most women nag too much	_____	_____
4.	Battering is found mainly among low-income families, because of money problems	_____	_____
5.	Is it rape when a husband forces his wife to have sex?	_____	_____
6.	A man should make the big decisions in a marriage	_____	_____
7.	Men are abused by women as often as women are by men, it's just not reported as much	_____	_____
8.	When children are beaten, it's generally because they have a behavior problem	_____	_____
9.	Violence happens in relatively few teenage dating relationships	_____	_____
10.	It's natural for boys to be aggressive	_____	_____
11.	Some girls like to be hit	_____	_____
12.	One out of four girls is sexually assaulted before age 18	_____	_____
13.	One out of six boys is sexually assaulted before age 18	_____	_____
14.	If a boy is sexually assaulted, it's usually by an adult woman	_____	_____
15.	If a girl stays in a relationship with someone who hits her, it's her own fault	_____	_____

(continued)

(Teen Program Posttest on Family/Teen Violence, continued)

16. When is it OK for a boy to hit a girl?

17. Why do some women stay in battering relationships?

18. Why do some men hit their partners?

19. If you or someone you know have parents in a violent relationship, where can you go to get help?

20. If you or someone you know is in a relationship with any violence in it now, where can you go to get help?

21. What advice can you give to a friend who comes from a home where violence is happening?

22. How can you improve your relationships with your friends based on what you've heard from us in the past few days?

Program Evaluation

1. What I liked about the presentation was:

2. What I learned from the presentation was:

3. What could be improved is:

4. What I still need information about is:

THIS SPACE FOR YOUR ADDRESS

Participant Evaluation

Name_____ Age_____ Phone_____

Teacher_____ Date_____

Write what you like, didn't like, want more of, and learned from our group/class on violence. Feel free to say what you really would like us to know. Thanks for all your help!

Things I liked: Things I didn't like:

Things I want more of: Things I learned:

If you or someone you know is in a relationship with any violence in it now, where can you go to get help?

How can you improve your relationships with your friends based upon what you've heard from us?

Would you like to hear more about the women's group on violence-free relationships we are offering at your school?   Y   N

THIS SPACE FOR YOUR ADDRESS

Student Survey

Anonymous

Age_____   Grade_____   Male/Female   Date_____

Thank you for answering these questions. Please do not sign your name.

1.   What do you like most about your family?

2.   What do you like least about your family?

3.   If you could change one thing about your life, what would that be?

4.   Do you know anyone who has been molested, beaten, or raped? Have you? Can you describe what happened?

5.   Describe briefly a situation in which you felt unsafe. Were you abused or afraid of being abused? What did you do to get out of it?

6.   Who can you talk to about any of these issues?

7.   What topics would you like to discuss during the next six weeks?

8.   What questions do you have?

(Reprinted by permission of Marin Abused Women's Services)

THIS SPACE FOR YOUR ADDRESS

Follow-Up Teacher Evaluation

Several months ago, we gave presentations on family and dating violence to your students. Please take a moment to give us an assessment of our long-term effect and what we need to do in the future. Thanks for your help!

1.   Your evaluation of the presentation at the time it happened:

   Things I liked: Things I didn't like:

   Things I want more of :   Things I learned:

2.   One way the presentation has affected you over the long term:

(continued)

(Follow-Up Teacher Evaluation, continued)

3. One way the presentation has NOT affected you over the long term:

4. A change in or long-term effect on your male students:

5. A change in or long-term effect on your female students:

6. How relationships between women and men in your class have changed since our presentation, and how they've not changed:

7. Your strongest recommendations for our project next year:

Thanks for your consideration. We look forward to working with you again.

THIS SPACE FOR YOUR ADDRESS

RELATED RESOURCES

**To do the three-day high school presentation outlined
in Section 4 you will need the video "MY GIRL . . . "**

"My Girl" was written and produced by Allan Creighton, along with the actors. A companion to HELPING TEENS STOP VIOLENCE, it shows how six-teen teenagers deal with two incidents of dating violence among their friends on a high school campus. In the process, young women disclose personal experiences of abuse and speak out to young men who finally intervene. Includes a curriculum guide.

Viewing time: 60 minutes ... VHS format ... $95.00

To order the video send $95.00 (plus tax in California) to:

> BATTERED WOMEN'S ALTERNATIVES
> P.O. Box 6406
> Concord, CA 94524

MEN'S WORK: How to Stop the Violence That Tears Our Lives Apart
by Paul Kivel.

Using the unique program at the Oakland Men's Project as a basis, this book describes an extraordinary approach to stopping male violence. The key is understanding and evading the cultural forces that box men in and often reward them for violent behavior. Through exercises, thought-provoking questions, and intense self-examination, MEN'S WORK helps men learn new rules and new roles in personal relationships and in the world at large.

> To order **MEN'S WORK**, contact the Hazelden Foundation
> Tel. 1-800-328-9000.

> Other resource books from Hunter House
> are listed on the following pages.

RESOURCES FOR EDUCATORS AND COUNSELORS

‚HOOL CRISIS MANAGEMENT: A Team Training Guide
by Kendall Johnson, Ph.D.

Written for school professionals—administrators, psychologists, counselors, and crisis response team members—this detailed guide goes beyond introductory trauma theory to give practical applications, specific procedures, and proven strategies for managing crisis situations in schools. Written simply and directly, it bridges the gap between theory and the real world of school operations. Includes 78 full-page charts that may be copied to make overhead transparencies.

192 pages ... 78 illustrations ... $15.95 preview edition ... $19.95 soft cover ... available December 1992 (preview edition available now)

RESPONDING TO CRISIS: A Planning Guide for Schools
by Kendall Johnson, Ph.D.

School personnel need techniques to evaluate a crisis situation, administer interventions, and return the school to stability. This guide will help school administrators develop an orchestrated response to meet the urgent needs of their students, explain children's reactions to crisis, and list objectives to help schools stabilize classroom learning environments.

98 pages ... $14.95 soft cover ... available January 1993

TRAUMA IN THE LIVES OF CHILDREN: Crisis and Stress Management
Techniques for Counselors and Other Professionals by Kendall Johnson, Ph.D.

Children may suffer trauma at any age: from a natural disaster, violence in the home, or seeing a shooting at school. If not properly handled, the trauma will have lasting effects on the child's development. In this practical book for professionals who deal with children in crisis, Kendall Johnson provides effective guidelines to prepare for and handle a crisis, and identify traumatized children who need help.

256 pages ... $15.95 soft cover

HUMAN RIGHTS FOR CHILDREN by the Amnesty International Human Rights for Children Committee.

No effort seems more appropriate to promoting peace and respect in our society than helping children develop an early awareness of their own human rights and the rights of others. This manual of curriculum activities for children ages three through twelve teaches children their universal rights and encourages self-worth, multicultural awareness, and empathy for others. **With illustrations by Marsha Sinetar.**

96 pages ... 12 illustrations ... soft cover $10.95 ... spiral edition $12.95

EVERYONE CAN WRITE: A Teaching Guide to Life Story Writing
by Bernard Selling.

Based on the method outlined in the author's book WRITING FROM WITHIN, this curriculum guide shows educators how to teach students *of all ages* to write using their own life experiences. The techniques inspire even the youngest writers to enjoy—not fear—writing. The book emphasizes the importance of supportive, non-judgmental group feedback, and contains curriculum outlines for early elementary school to high school and adult school.

176 pages ... 18 illustrations ... $14.95 soft cover ... available February 1993

See last page for our order form

OTHER RESOURCES FOR TEENS

TURNING YOURSELF AROUND: Self-Help Strategies for Troubled Teens
by Kendall Johnson, Ph.D.

This is a support book for young adults, ages 15–20, who are going through 12-step programs. It follows the stories of three young people—one a bulimic, another an alcoholic, and the third a relationship addict. We see their individual problems, personal needs, and different stages of recovery. The book provides overviews of the issues, followed by provocative questions and exercises that will help all teens deal with life issues. A pullout guide for parents, teachers, or counselors is included.

224 pages ... soft cover ... $9.95

FEELING GREAT: Reaching Out to the World, Reaching in to Yourself—Without Drugs by Nancy Levinson & Joanne Rocklin, Ph.D.

A highly positive book for teenagers who are facing the pressures of social drug and alcohol use. Newly updated for the nineties, this activity-filled book speaks to both younger and older teens, and shows how the real, natural highs only come from being deeply involved in life and the world. An invaluable resource for working with drug-related issues.

112 pages ... soft cover ... $7.95

RAISING EACH OTHER: A Book for Teens and Parents by Jeanne Brondino and the Parent/Teen Book Group.

Written by teens and based on high school essays and parent interviews, this book is a dialogue between generations about trust, freedom, responsibility, drugs, sex, religion, and more. A valuable guide for both sides, RAISING EACH OTHER shows how, through a new spirit of communication, we can help each other learn, grow, and love.

"An endearing and revealing work"—Studs Terkel

160 pages ... soft cover ... $8.95

SAFE DIETING FOR TEENS by Linda Ojeda, Ph.D.

Linda Ojeda outlines the dangers of yo-yo dieting and other eating disorders, while offering young women a positive alternative to fad diets and weight-loss centers. Her common sense approach combines sensible eating with raising the metabolism rate and building muscle to keep weight down permanently. Resources include a calorie count chart for typical foods, a removable parents guide, and calendars to track calorie intake. With this guide, a shape-conscious teen can escape from the trauma of constant dieting, and restore eating to the simple, positive, and natural part of life it was meant to be.

128 pages ... soft cover ... $7.95

PMS: PREMENSTRUAL SYNDROME: A Guide for Young Women by Gilda Berger.

The *only* book on PMS written expressly for *teenage* women. Explains what PMS is, its physical and psychological symptoms, and medical and self-help treatments. This book—especially useful for parents of teenage girls—answers the questions: How do I know if I have PMS? What can I do to feel better? Who do I talk to? Will it ever go away?

96 pages ... soft cover ... 3rd Edition ... $7.95

Prices subject to change without notice
See over for ordering and discounts

ORDER FORM

NAME

ADDRESS

CITY/STATE   ZIP

COUNTRY (outside USA)   POSTAL CODE

TITLE	QTY	PRICE	TOTAL
Helping Teens Stop Violence (soft cover)		@ $ 11.95	
Helping Teens Stop Violence (spiral)		@ $ 14.95	
Everyone Can Write		@ $ 14.95	
Feeling Great		@ $ 7.95	
Human Rights for Children (soft cover)		@ $ 10.95	
PMS: A Guide for Young Women		@ $ 7.95	
Raising Each Other		@ $ 8.95	
Responding to Crisis		@ $ 14.95	
Safe Dieting For Teens		@ $ 7.95	
School Crisis Management (soft cover)		@ $ 19.95	
Trauma in the Lives of Children		@ $ 15.95	
Turning Yourself Around		@ $ 9.95	

Shipping costs:
*First book: $2.00
($3.00 for Canada)
Each additional book:
$.50 ($1.00 for
Canada)*
*For UPS rates and
bulk orders call us at
(510) 865-5282*

TOTAL
Less discount @_____%
TOTAL COST OF BOOKS
Calif. residents add sales tax
Shipping & handling
TOTAL ENCLOSED
Please pay in U.S. funds only

( )

❑ Check   ❑ Money Order   ❑ Visa   ❑ M/C

Card # _____ Exp date _____

Signature _____

Complete and mail to:
Hunter House Inc., Publishers
P.O. Box 2914, Alameda CA 94501-0914
Phone (510) 865-5282 Fax (510) 865-4295

❑ Check here to receive our book catalog